I0032822

THE ASIAN DEVELOPMENT BANK'S KNOWLEDGE MANAGEMENT IN ACTION

VISION, LEARNING, AND COLLABORATION

DECEMBER 2021

ASIAN DEVELOPMENT BANK

ADB

Contents

Foreword

Knowledge management has always been intertwined with the work of the Asian Development Bank (ADB). How that came to be is a story that deserves to be told. It begins with a vision as old as the institution itself: to create a bank that is not just a source of development funding, but also a valued source of applied expertise and knowledge.

Since its founding in 1966, ADB's commitment to build a knowledge base out of its experience steadily increased and led to the creation of a knowledge management framework in 2004. This contributed to shaping a provision in Strategy 2020 that ensured ADB would play a larger role in harnessing knowledge to promote development across Asia and the Pacific. Today, our knowledge management is guided by Strategy 2030, with a call-to-action for ADB to solidify its role as knowledge solutions provider. Our Knowledge Management Action Plan 2021–2025 adds substance to this call. We work closely with ADB's developing members to back our lending with knowledge. At the country level, our country knowledge plans, with each country director designated as knowledge custodian, help strategic planning, implementation, and monitoring of the knowledge operations.

Despite the region's profound economic transformation—with many countries now middle-income, and hundreds of millions of people lifted out of poverty—many critical challenges remain. Countering these challenges would not be possible for developing Asia and the Pacific without harnessing the power of knowledge. The coronavirus disease (COVID-19) pandemic has been unparalleled in reminding us of this point—accelerating and diversifying trends in knowledge management. Pandemic responses show that a country and its people can be only as effective as the knowledge they harness, share, and apply. The same pertains to organizations. ADB is using a combination of culture, systems, and process changes for knowledge management to effectively address the pandemic across sectors, agencies, and countries.

This book is the story of ADB's journey through various stages of our knowledge management process from 1966 until today. We aspire to be the most valued knowledge advisor to our developing members; a vibrant learning organization that encourages collaboration; and a platform for sharing ideas, knowledge, and experience.

In 2019, we began capturing knowledge solutions in the form of brief case studies to demonstrate how we worked with our countries to address development challenges. We also started collecting stories and case studies to document how innovation helps improve the quality of our investment products. It is from these case studies, shared by ADB staff, that you will see the depth and breadth of how ADB and our developing members jointly create knowledge solutions. I invite you to delve into these knowledge solutions and journey across the rich knowledge landscape of ADB and developing Asia and the Pacific.

The journey will not stop here.

Amid the region's ever-evolving development challenges, ADB will continue to harness and manage knowledge with its members for their green, resilient, inclusive, and sustainable development.

Bambang Susantono
Vice-President for Knowledge Management and
Sustainable Development
Asian Development Bank

Acknowledgments

Production managers:
Susann Roth and Vivek Raman

Authors:
Vivek Raman, Pronita Agrawal, Mary Jane F. Carangal-San Jose, Ashwath Dasarathy, John Mercurio, and Josephine J. Aquino.

The following provided valuable input in the preparation of the book:
Linda Arthur, Imelda Baleta, Mc Reynald S. Banderlipe II, Daniel Luis Beran, Maribeth Cesicar-Sanvictores, Kar Joon Fan, Sarah Pahwa, Suveer Singh, Sonoko Sunayama, and the various project teams for each featured knowledge solution

Special thanks:
Bambang Susantono, Vice-President for Knowledge Management and Sustainable Development for his time and inputs to the conceptualization of this book

Manuscript editors:
Jane Parry and Maria Theresa Mercado

Layout design:
Insomniac Design, Inc.

Abbreviations

ACGF	ASEAN Catalytic Green Finance
ADB	Asian Development Bank
ADF	Asian Development Fund
AEIR	Asian Economic Integration Report
AFD	Agence Française de Développement
AICOE	ASEAN Infrastructure Centre of Excellence
ARW	Anticorruption and Respect at Work
ASEAN	Association of Southeast Asian Nations
BETDP	Basic Education Textbook Development Project
COVID-19	coronavirus disease
CPS	country partnership strategy
CSF	countercyclical support facility
DMC	developing member country
DOE	Department of Environment
DWASA	Dhaka Water Supply and Sewerage Authority
ECA	ecologically critical area
ERCD	Economic Research and Regional Cooperation Department
FFEWS	flood forecasting and early warning system
FMiD	Financial Management Information Dashboard
GCE	General Certificate of Education
GCF	Green Climate Fund
GDP	gross domestic product
GIS	geographical information system
GMS	Greater Mekong Subregion
ICT	information and communication technology
IED	Independent Evaluation Department
IMF	International Monetary Fund
INDC	Intended Nationally Determined Contribution
IT	information technology
ITD	Information Technology Department
JFPR	Japan Fund for Poverty Reduction
KEIIP	Kolkata Environment Improvement Investment Program

Abbreviations

KMAP	Knowledge Management Action Plan
KMC	Kolkata Municipal Corporation
KSSC	Knowledge Sharing and Services Center
MAKE	Most Admired Knowledge Enterprise
MOU	memorandum of understanding
MOUD	Ministry of Urban Development
NSO	National Statistics Office
NUC	Nauru Utilities Corporation
OAI	Office of Anticorruption and Integrity
OGC	Office of the General Counsel
PEFA	Public Expenditure and Financial Accountability
PPFD	Procurement, Portfolio, and Financial Management Department
PRC	People's Republic of China
RBL	results-based loan
RCI	regional cooperation and integration
RPC	Regional Processing Centre
RSDD	Regional Sustainable Development Department
SDG	Sustainable Development Goal
SERD	Southeast Asia Department
SGDF	Shandong Green Development Fund
SME	small and medium-sized enterprises
SOE	state-owned enterprise
SPC	Secretariat of the Pacific Community
STG	sector and thematic group
TA	technical assistance
TANGEDCO	Tamil Nadu Generation & Distribution Company
TSCFP	Trade and Supply Chain Finance Program
TVET	technical and vocational education and training
UCCRTF	Urban Climate Change Resilience Trust Fund
UHC	universal health coverage
UNICEF	United Nations Children's Fund
WHO	World Health Organization

1966–2004
Stage 1:
The Vision

2005–2009
Stage 2:
Expansion

2010–2014
Stage 3:
Steps Forward, Steps Back

The Asian Development Bank's Knowledge Management Journey:
Decades of Learning, Engagement, and Vision

The first President of the Asian Development Bank (ADB), Takeshi Watanabe, often emphasized that the bank was an institution that "learns before it teaches." He characterized ADB as a "family doctor," meaning it had expert knowledge that it used for good. From the very beginning, ADB has complemented its lending services with knowledge support as a key development resource.[1] In fact, the ADB Charter directs ADB to provide knowledge support in the form of technical assistance (TA) to developing member countries (DMCs), in addition to financing.[2] Now, the Knowledge Management Action Plan (KMAP) 2021–2025 describes ADB as a regional advisor that is able to provide tailored knowledge solutions to DMCs, the latest stage in a decades-long evolution of knowledge management at ADB.

2015–2021
Stage 4:
Regained Momentum

Stage 5
Looking Back for Lessons Learned, Looking Ahead to the Future of Knowledge Management

---

[1] McCawley, P. 2017. *Banking on the Future of Asia and the Pacific: 50 Years of the Asian Development Bank.* Manila: Asian Development Bank.

[2] ADB. 1966. *Agreement Establishing the Asian Development Bank.* Manila.

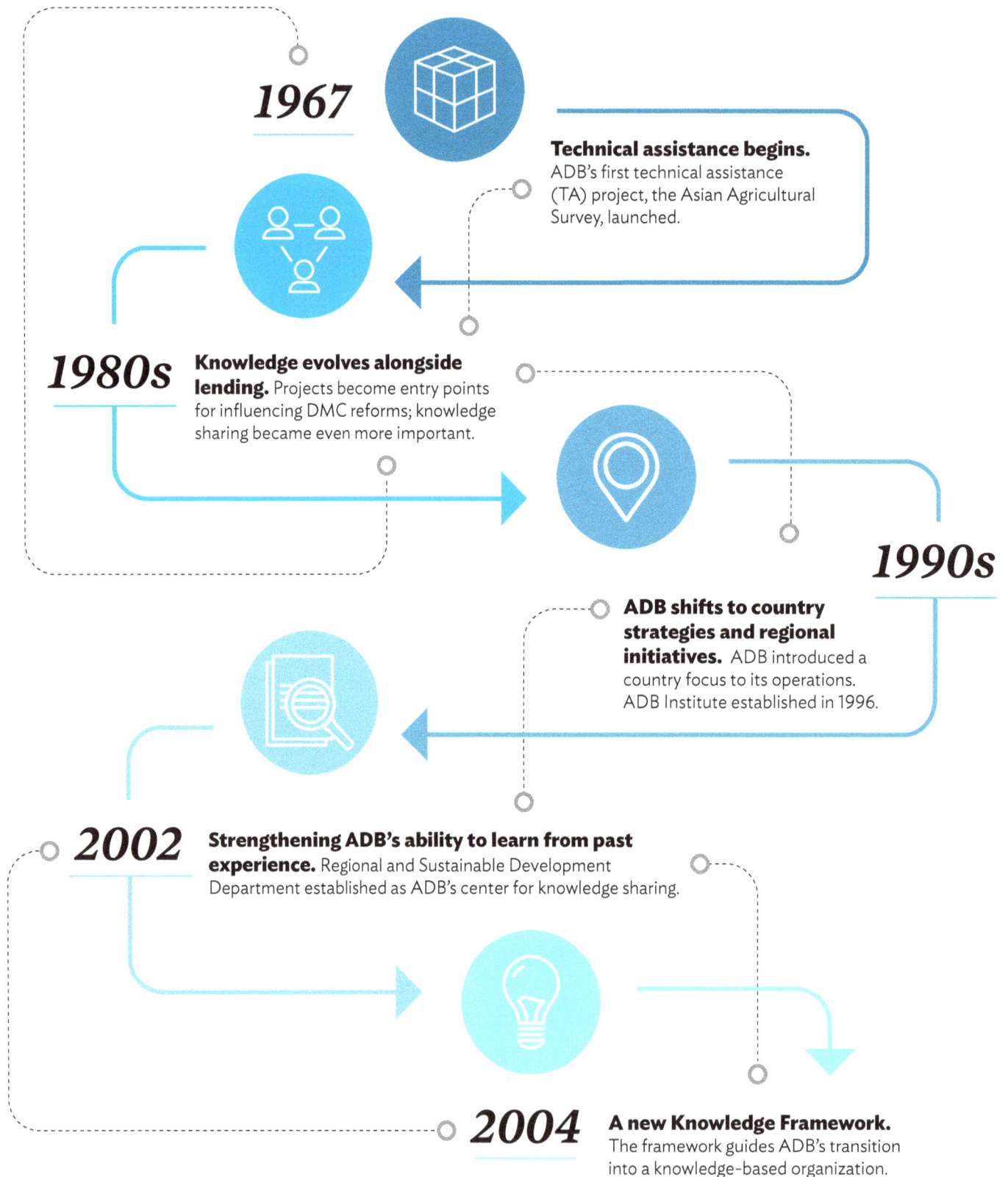

1967

Technical assistance begins.
ADB's first technical assistance
(TA) project, the Asian Agricultural
Survey, launched.

1980s

**Knowledge evolves alongside
lending.** Projects become entry points
for influencing DMC reforms; knowledge
sharing became even more important.

1990s

**ADB shifts to country
strategies and regional
initiatives.** ADB introduced a
country focus to its operations.
ADB Institute established in 1996.

2002

**Strengthening ADB's ability to learn from past
experience.** Regional and Sustainable Development
Department established as ADB's center for knowledge sharing.

2004

A new Knowledge Framework.
The framework guides ADB's transition
into a knowledge-based organization.

from **2005** to **2007**

01
Monitoring knowledge management effectiveness
2005: ADB began staff surveys of its Knowledge Management Implementation Framework.

02
2005: Knowledge Management Center formed

Under the new center, knowledge products and services output—books, reports, journals, briefs, working papers, training materials, and multimedia content—increased yearly.

03
The creation of new communities of practice
Communities across a wide range of themes and sectors created.

from **2007** to **2009**

04
Knowledge solutions seen as a driver of change
Country diagnostic studies show need for more understanding of constraints faced by DMCs.

05
DMCs demand for technical assistance increasing
Strategy 2020 declares ADB must deploy cutting-edge knowledge and technical services to complement financing.

06
Knowledge Management Action Plan 2009–2011

This plan laid out a pragmatic approach aimed to sharpen ADB's knowledge focus, empower the communities of practice, and strengthen external knowledge partnerships.

from 2010 to 2012

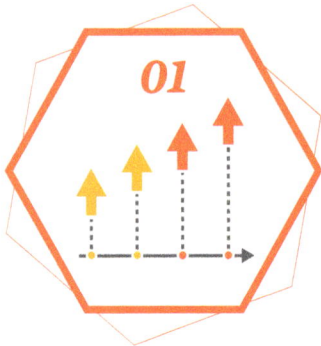

01

Knowledge Management Action Plan in full swing
Under the plan, the aggregate budget for communities of practice increased tenfold, to $1 million; they became integral partners in peer review and recruitment.

02

Stronger communities of practice, country partnerships
Communities of practice grew from 10 to 13; country partnership strategy processes were streamlined to strengthen knowledge management and better align with client needs.

from 2012 to 2014

03

ADB's first Knowledge Forum
The forum built stronger connections between ADB departments, and the Knowledge Sharing and Services Center was restructured to strengthen knowledge management coordination.

04

Affirming the importance of "One ADB"
In 2014, the first Knowledge Operations Review Meeting brought knowledge management discussions to the level of ADB operations.

from 2015 to 2018

01

Midterm review of Strategy 2030 points the way

ADB's knowledge management journey picked up speed with the introduction of the country knowledge plan, designating the country director as knowledge custodian.

02

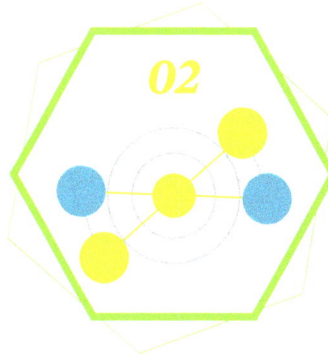

The shift to sector and thematic groups

The sector and thematic groups empowered to work closely with sector committees in ADB's regional departments.

03

Strategy 2030 strengthens ADB as a knowledge provider

Need for high-level strategic guidance on knowledge management and integration with finance and partnerships recognized.

from 2018 to 2021

04

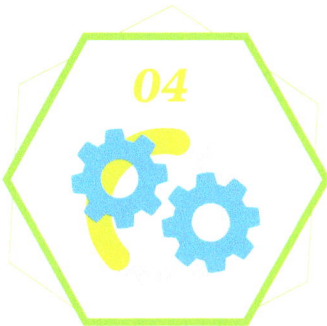

Work begins on ADB's innovation framework

While knowledge management was seen in previous years as a tool to increase efficiency, the focus shifted from managing knowledge to implementing innovation.

05

A plan for collaboration, relevance, and impact

The new Knowledge Management Action Plan 2021–2025 determines concrete actions to continue to align knowledge management with Strategy 2030.

Technical assistance (TA) operations aim to improve the capabilities of ADB's developing member countries (DMCs) to formulate, design, implement, and operate development projects and sector lending. TA comes in many forms, including sector studies, surveys, workshops, seminars, and training. The first recorded TA was the Asian Agricultural Survey launched in 1967. This was the basis of a plan of action to address agricultural problems in the region, and it demonstrated the use of TA as the primary platform for providing knowledge assistance to DMCs.

ADB's role as a knowledge expert has evolved alongside its role as a lender. During the 1980s, the bank evolved from supporting projects on a case-by-case basis to implementing projects as an entry point for influencing sector policy reforms in the DMCs. ADB then went on to introduce a country focus to its operations in the 1990s. At around this time, ADB also started to develop country strategies and to work under regional initiatives, such as those in the Greater Mekong Subregion.[3] Internally, the ADB Institute (ADBI) was established in 1996 to broaden the reach of ADB's evidence-based policy work (see page 18 for details.)

As the bank's focus evolved, from project to sector, then to country and region, a growing need for bespoke knowledge solutions became clear. However, as ADB grew, it inevitably became bigger and more complex. An unintended consequence of this was that corporate culture became more impersonal. It became increasingly difficult to have spontaneous interactions with colleagues that could foster innovation, debate, and knowledge sharing. At the same time, there was no system in place to capture, store, share, and reuse knowledge. Clearly, the bank needed to strengthen its knowledge management to sustain its growth.

The process of strengthening knowledge management unfolded organically, and as a result it took time. It was more than 3 decades after its creation that ADB formally set out its aim of becoming a knowledge institution, with the launch of the Long-Term Strategic Framework, 2001–2015. For ADB to become a learning institution, the framework required it to "develop the capacity to learn quickly from its own operational experiences and those of its development partners, and to disseminate such experience in the form of best practices among DMCs, ADB staff, and the development partners."[4] This articulated for the first time the role knowledge would play in ADB's overarching goal of poverty reduction. It stated ADB's vision to become a primary source of development knowledge in Asia and the Pacific.[5] This ability to learn from past experience was evident in 2002 when the Economic Research and Regional Cooperation Department (ERCD) introduced the Economic Analysis Retrospectives to improve project quality-at-entry, and assess the quality of the economic analysis of ADB projects.

The 2004 Knowledge Management Framework provided direction and guidance for knowledge management, broadly defined as "the way organizations create, capture, enhance, and reuse knowledge to achieve organizational objectives."[6] Covering organizational culture, business processes, management systems and information technology (IT) solutions, the framework guided ADB's transition

---

[3] ADB. 2009. ADB Reflections and Beyond. Manila

[4] ADB. 2001. Moving the Poverty Reduction Agenda Forward in Asia and the Pacific: The Long-term Strategic Framework of the Asian Development Bank (2001-2015). Manila.

[5] ADB. 2004. Enhancing the Fight Against Poverty in Asia and the Pacific. Manila.

[6] ADB. 2004. Knowledge Management in ADB. Manila.

into a knowledge-based organization until ADB's first knowledge management action plan was formulated in 2009.

With these policies in place, ADB then moved to address specific knowledge management challenges, including organization and leadership, processes, and IT. As an initial step to facilitate the flow of knowledge across different departments, the Regional and Sustainable Development Department (RSDD) had been established in 2002 to be ADB's center for knowledge sharing between sector and thematic networks or committees, two of which originally resided in ERCD. That year, 19 networks were created across 9 sectors and themes. However, it became apparent that they were poorly organized, and dogged by overly restrictive membership, ambiguous responsibilities, hierarchical structures, and inadequate funding. Clearly, senior leadership support was going to be crucial in enabling the culture of genuine knowledge sharing to become embedded in the institution. In 2003, ADB added a fourth senior leadership role, vice-president for Knowledge Management. Since then, this vice-president has overseen the strategic coherence of ADB operations, and coordinates sector and thematic policies for knowledge sharing and learning.

An organization's knowledge management relies on its people, and the organizational reforms were complemented by a new human resource strategy in 2004. This established an ADB-wide competency framework to enhance learning and knowledge sharing within the bank. Five core competencies were required of staff members and new recruits:

- client orientation,
- achieving results,
- working together,
- learning and knowledge sharing, and
- application of technical knowledge and skills.

Meanwhile, knowledge management infrastructure got a much-needed boost in 2004, with the approval of the second Information Systems and Technology Strategy. This led to the creation of ADB's enterprise-wide repository, the Electronic Storage and Retrieval System (eSTAR).[7] By 2005, the groundwork had been laid for an expansion of ADB's knowledge management capabilities.

> " *To respond to evolving challenges, ADB must become a learning institution maximizing the use of its vast knowledge and drawing upon resources, skills, and expertise both inside and outside the organization.* **Long-Term Strategic Framework of ADB, 2001–2015**

---

[7]   ADB. 2018. *ADB 2030 Digital Agenda: Social Capital Expenditure Requirements for 2019–2030.* Manila

From 2005 to 2012, ADB commissioned staff surveys of its Knowledge Management Implementation Framework, using a customized tool, Most Admired Knowledge Enterprises (MAKE). MAKE covered eight recognized knowledge performance dimensions to determine overarching knowledge management trends at ADB.

The surveys revealed a lack of consistency across key knowledge performance dimensions: knowledge-driven culture, senior management leadership, enterprise-wide knowledge collaboration, organizational learning, intellectual capital, and improved stakeholder's standard of living.[8] ADB used the insights from these surveys to continue to track its progress in managing knowledge, improve synergy within the organization's knowledge management efforts, and establish the right structures, roles, and functions for effective knowledge management.[9]

In 2005, the Knowledge Management Center was formed, primarily to develop knowledge management tools. With the center in place, knowledge products and services increased fivefold between 2004 and 2011. From year to year there was a substantial increase in the output of books, reports, journals, briefs, working papers, training materials, and multimedia content posted on ADB.org.

ADB's progress toward effective knowledge management, and ensuring learning was integral to operations, was in tune with Strategy 2020, released in 2008, which was a rallying cry for ADB to play a bigger part in harnessing knowledge solutions to promote development across Asia and the Pacific.

One of the key drivers of change under Strategy 2020 was knowledge solutions, i.e., knowledge products and services that help solve development problems in DMCs. The strategy highlighted knowledge solutions as a driver of change. Such solutions require a broad understanding of development constraints faced by DMCs, which has been the subject of ERCD's country diagnostic studies since 2007.

The sector and thematic communities and networks were renamed and aggregated into 10 communities of practice in 2005, covering education, energy, environment, finance, gender and social development, governance, health, regional cooperation, transport, and water. With increasing DMC demand for finance and TA, Strategy 2020 declared that it "must continue to help DMCs gain access to long-term funds at reasonable terms, manage risks, take collective action, and deploy cutting-edge knowledge and technical services to complement financing."[10]

The sector and thematic communities and networks were renamed and aggregated into 10 communities of practice in 2005, covering education, energy, environment, finance, gender and social development, governance, health, regional cooperation, transport, and water.

[8]   Most Admired Knowledge Enterprise Survey Reports from 2005–2008.

[9]   ADB. 2007. *Special Evaluation Study on Long-Term Strategic Framework: Lessons from Implementation 2001–2006*. Manila.

[10] ADB. 2008. *Strategy 2020: The Long-Term Strategic Framework of the Asian Development Bank 2008–2020*. Manila

> *"Strategy 2020 will also require institutional change... ADB will adapt its organizational structure to new and expanded products and services, particularly in private sector operations, financial services, knowledge management, and environmental operations."*
> **Midterm Review of Strategy 2020**

The RSDD developed Learning for Change Primers to train staff on IT, the essentials of successful communities of practice, knowledge management, building a learning organization, and improving the design of knowledge partnerships.[11]

By the far the most significant milestone in this period was the approval of the first KMAP, for 2009–2011.[12] This laid out a pragmatic, step-by-step approach aimed "to sharpen the knowledge focus of ADB operations, empower the communities of practice, strengthen external knowledge partnership, and further enhance staff learning and skills development."

This was progress indeed, but there was still a need to facilitate access for DMC stakeholders to knowledge services through an easily searchable repository of knowledge solutions.

---

[11] ADB. 2011. *Guidelines for Knowledge Partnerships*. Manila.
[12] ADB. 2009. *Enhancing Knowledge Management Under Strategy 2020*. Manila.

STAGE THREE:
Steps Forward, Steps Back (2010-2014)

By 2010, the knowledge management performance staff surveys revealed steady improvement across all dimensions, but this process leveled off in subsequent years (Figure 1). To address this, recommended reforms included

- clarifying the functions and roles of the communities of practice and resident missions in knowledge work,
- strengthening the mainstreaming of knowledge work in projects,
- improving incentives for knowledge work, and
- increasing budget for staff development and knowledge sharing.[13]

Figure 1: Most Admired Knowledge Enterprise Survey Results, 2005–2011

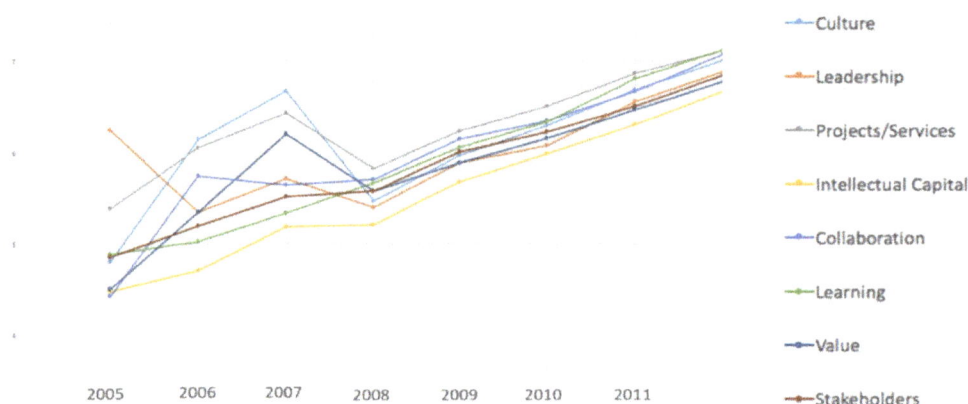

Source: Assessment of ADB's Knowledge Management Implementation Framework Surveys, 2005–2011.

Figure 2: Communities of Practice in 2011

Agriculture, Rural Development, and Food Security	75
Education	41
Energy	171
Environment	110
Financial Sector Development	196
Gender Equity	100
Social Development and Poverty	246
Governance and Public Management	93
Health	24
Regional Cooperation and Integration	26
Transport	147
Urban	115
Water	214
Total CoP Membership	**1,558**

CoP = Communities of Practice.
Source: Asian Development Bank. 2011. 2011 Survey of ADB-Hosted Communities of Practice Final Report. Manila.

Once the KMAP 2009–2011 implementation was in full swing, most of these issues were addressed. Under the plan, the aggregate budget for communities of practice increased tenfold, to $10,000,000, and they became integral partners in peer review processes and staff performance review and recruitment. The value of communities of practice was enhanced, and the number increased from 10 to 13 (Figure 2). Under the KMAP, country partnership strategy (CPS) processes were streamlined to strengthen knowledge management mainstreaming work and better align projects with client needs.[14]

---

[13] Serrat, O. 2011. Surveying Communities of Practice. Knowledge Solutions. No. 104. Manila: Asian Development Bank.
ADB. 2009. Streamlining Country Partnership Strategies. Manila; various Most Admired Knowledge Enterprise Survey reports; McCawley, P. 2017. Banking on the Future of Asia and the Pacific: 50 Years of the Asian Development Bank. Manila.

[14] ADB. 2009. Country Partnership Strategy Responding To The New Aid Architecture. Manila.

A new human resources policy document, Our People Strategy 2010, demonstrated ADB's strong commitment to knowledge management by defining core knowledge competencies to guide staff retention, recruitment, and development. These were

- application of technical knowledge and skills,
- leadership and strategic thinking,
- communication and knowledge sharing,
- change and innovation,
- achieving results and problem solving,
- client orientation, and
- working together.

To lock in support for knowledge sharing and teamwork, the KMAP Results Framework, approved in March 2010, was incorporated in the Work Program and Budget Framework. Furthermore, Human Resources recognized teamwork success stories and instituted an award system for teamwork and multidisciplinary work units. This all helped the cause of effective knowledge management.

Implementation of the second phase of the Information Systems and Technology Strategy continued, with new collaboration mechanisms for cross-departmental and multidisciplinary knowledge generation and sharing. The bank initiated several projects to improve information access and retrieval, including the development of an intranet for easier access to community of practice web pages and ADB databases such as ERCD's data library and database of DMC statistics; knowledge management applications (KMApps) for knowledge sharing, capture, and dissemination; and Mapview for improved spatial information use.

To further maximize the gains from these improved strategic, human resource, and IT directions, ADB consolidated three specialized knowledge units, the Economics and Research Department (currently ERCD), the Office of Regional Economic Integration, and the RSDD, under an expanded vice-presidency for knowledge management and sustainable development. This consolidation helped formalize the key role of knowledge management within the bank.

Other initiatives further strengthened knowledge management within the bank, including the establishment of the Knowledge Forum in 2012. Chaired by the President, the forum aimed to build stronger connections between ADB departments, including the ADBI, and avoid duplication of efforts. In addition, the Knowledge Sharing and Services Center was restructured to replace the Knowledge Management Center and strengthen knowledge management coordination and guidance.

In 2011 and 2012, ADB received the Asian MAKE Award for its commendable performance in collaborative enterprise-wide knowledge sharing. ADB was one of four public organizations out of 20 winners to have been chosen for this award by a panel of Fortune 500 senior executives and internationally recognized knowledge management experts.

By 2013, the push for knowledge management reforms started to slow down, but there was still progress toward improving the internal system, including the approval of the Knowledge Management Directions and Action Plan 2013–2015 and the third phase of the Information Systems and Technology Strategy. Both initiatives focused on enhancing information and communication technology (ICT) systems for better internal and external stakeholder communication and collaboration. On the human resources side, a recommendation that knowledge contribution be included in staff performance evaluation was approved, and international staff were strategically reassigned to promote knowledge sharing.

In 2014, the first Knowledge Operations Review Meeting affirmed the importance of "One ADB," and brought knowledge management discussions to the level of ADB operations. The Midterm Review of Strategy 2020 was conducted in the same year to "prepare ADB to meet the challenges of a transforming Asia and the Pacific."

"

There was a change when knowledge management became part of performance evaluation, but this was not enough. More incentives were needed to make people do more knowledge management, make it part of their day-to-day job.

STAGE FOUR:
Regained Momentum (2015–2021)

Strategy 2030, released in 2018, states that

> *ADB will strengthen its role as a knowledge provider. ADB will work closely with DMCs to identify their needs and produce the most relevant knowledge products and services. It will incentivize staff to integrate the best available knowledge with financing and institutional capacity building throughout the operational cycle. ADB will proactively engage in research, provide high quality policy advice to DMCs, and strengthen DMCs' institutional capacity in addressing development issues.*

ADB's research is showcased annually during ERCD's Economists' Forum. This raises the profile and quality of ADB's research, aligns it with Strategy 2030 priorities, shares knowledge across the bank, and facilitates collaborative research work.

In 2015, after a midterm review of Strategy 2020, ADB's knowledge management journey picked up speed, with the introduction of the country knowledge plan, designating the country director as knowledge custodian. Each country knowledge plan reflects a DMC's knowledge priorities considering its specific circumstances and needs. Since then, a country knowledge plan has been appended to each CPS, and is operationalized through a pipeline of knowledge products and services reflected in the country operations and business plan.

The Midterm Review of Strategy 2020 noted that majority of the DMCs were transitioning to middle-income status and thus had improved their institutional capacity, and their needs were diversifying.[15] As a result these DMCs were expecting ADB to respond to their changing needs.[16]

In 2014, ADB's then-President Takehiko Nakao announced his intention for ADB to become "stronger, better, and faster" and pressure mounted to really inculcate the vision of "One ADB" across departments and between ADB headquarters and its resident missions. Becoming a stronger knowledge institution meant ADB needed clearer, high-level strategic guidance on knowledge management, and a more systemic feedback mechanism for addressing the needs of DMCs.

In response to these challenges, in 2018 ADB implemented Strategy 2030, which aims to strengthen ADB's role as a knowledge provider. The strategy also promises to "incentivize staff to integrate the best available knowledge with financing and institutional capacity building throughout the operational cycle."[17] It highlights the bank's approach, which integrates finance, knowledge, and partnership in its operations.

To align their functions more closely with operations, the communities of practice were reconstituted into sector and thematic groups (STGs) in 2015. The STGs had more flexible budgets and have since been

---

[15] ADB. 2014. *Review of Medium-Term Strategy 2020: Meeting the Challenge of a Transforming Asia and the Pacific.* Manila.

[16] McCawley, P. 2017. *Banking on the Future of Asia and the Pacific: 50 Years of the Asian Development Bank.* Manila.

[17] ADB. 2018. *Strategy 2030, Achieving a Prosperous, Inclusive, Resilient and Sustainable Asia and the Pacific.* Manila.

empowered to work closely with sector committees in the bank's regional departments.

Several initiatives were introduced to improve knowledge management and sharing. Cross-department assignments were instigated through a mobility framework, staff exchanges, and short-term assignments. In 2016, flexible position management was introduced to optimize deployment of staff; enhance skills, knowledge sharing, and collaboration; and promote career and staff satisfaction. An experts' pool was introduced to complement staff competence in emerging project areas such as disaster risk finance and smart cities. At the same time, resident mission staff were expanded to foster country-focused operations. There was also an increasing focus on knowledge partnerships. An Independent Evaluation Department (IED) study on the effectiveness of partnerships led to the creation of the Partnership Toolbox in 2019 and the Partnership Portal in 2020. ICT modernization continued, incorporating new systems for nonsovereign operations and management of partner funds. The new ICT systems support ongoing improvements in knowledge management. Their resilience and agility were tested when the COVID-19 pandemic ushered in the new

normal of doing business remotely, requiring real-time collaboration during work-from-home arrangements.

Work on ADB's innovation framework started in 2018. While knowledge management was seen in previous years as a tool to increase efficiency, the focus shifted from managing knowledge to implementing innovation. In 2020, an IED special evaluation study highlighted a new set of focus areas including

- providing impactful knowledge solutions;
- increasing collaboration and reducing knowledge silos;
- enhancing relevance and quality of knowledge;
- building knowledge management capacity in resident missions and country teams; and
- optimizing the contribution and learning of staff, consultants, and partners to the organization.[18]

Drawing on these focus areas and building on other initiatives including operational reviews and the innovation framework, the new Knowledge Management Action Plan 2021–2025[19] determines concrete actions to continue to align knowledge management with Strategy 2030.

---

[18] ADB. 2020. *Knowledge Solutions for Development: An Evaluation of ADB's Readiness for Strategy 2030.*
[19] ADB. 2021. Knowledge Management Action Plan 2021–2025. Manila.

The bank's knowledge management journey is not yet complete, but the next stage is set, and is guided by the lessons of past endeavors. Here are six lessons learned:

Lesson 1. ADB's corporate strategies played a significant role in jumpstarting knowledge management reforms.

These strategies had a ripple effect in other significant aspects of the organization, such as people, processes, and ICT. ADB's corporate strategy, along with the KMAP, remain the most important documents articulating ADB's knowledge agenda.

Lesson 2. Knowledge management was borne out of client demand for solutions to development challenges.

Responding to clients' evolving needs is key to ADB maintaining its relevance as a development bank. This means continuously generating innovative solutions, adapting them from one setting to another, and adopting the right mix of proactive and reactive problem-solving strategies.

Lesson 3. ADB's capacity to respond to DMCs' demand for knowledge depends on the financial and human resources dedicated to knowledge management.

Sometimes competing priorities adversely affect the progress of knowledge management reforms, but financing for this crucial area of the bank's work must be protected. This includes investment in ICT infrastructure, which should allow a more efficient, bankwide, cross-sector, and cross-thematic knowledge capture, storage, retrieval, and reuse.

Lesson 4. Leadership and incentives matter.

High-level knowledge management guidance and direction raises awareness and brings people together to share knowledge. At the same time, staff need incentives to contribute to knowledge capital, and their efforts need to be recognized and rewarded.

Lesson 5. Evaluation is key to identifying issues, challenges, and areas of reform for knowledge management.

IED's evaluations of knowledge management within the bank are good springboards for developing solutions to improve ADB's knowledge processes. For example, experience showed that as ADB grew, it became harder to locate critical expertise. Understanding this points to a need for partnership tools that enable project teams to find out who knows what, within and outside the bank.

Lesson 6. Only a bankwide knowledge management policy can institutionalize the necessary processes across the bank.

Various knowledge management initiatives are being carried out in different departments, each following processes unique to them. A policy that will not only define roles and responsibilities, leadership, and incentives, but also integrate best practices from various departments into one coherent system will enable knowledge management to become assimilated within the bank's operations.

The Future of Knowledge Management at ADB

In the mid-1960s, when President Watanabe envisioned ADB's role as a family doctor, he did so in the era of doctor-knows-best medicine. Just as the doctor–patient relationship has evolved to become more collegial and collaborative, so too has ADB's approach to knowledge changed with the times. Being a family doctor means DMCs participate in diagnosing their development problems and find solutions to them together with ADB. At the same time, DMCs have become more demanding in terms of the experience and expertise they expect ADB to bring to the table.

ADB's evolving role means that it must now become the regional "advisor" that supports DMCs with bespoke solutions on their long-term sustainable development paths. The good news is the sheer volume of knowledge at ADB's disposal now compared to the early days of the bank represents an unprecedented opportunity to work together with DMCs and for ADB to achieve its vision of a prosperous, inclusive, resilient, and sustainable Asia and the Pacific. The ongoing challenge is how to marshal those resources to ensure that everyone in the organization relies not only on their own experience and expertise but can also quickly call upon that of anyone else at ADB. That ability hinges on a sound knowledge management action plan.

ADB's Knowledge Management Action Plan 2021–2025

The Knowledge Management Action Plan 2021–2025 will support Strategy 2030 to enable the bank to produce tailored knowledge solutions to DMCs. ADB's knowledge management journey will be guided by five key principles:

1. A differentiated approach: knowledge services across DMCs address different needs.
2. Balance: knowledge services that are demand and supply driven, top-down and bottom-up, contribute to sustainable development in DMCs.
3. Culture and learning: the importance of organizational culture and learning is recognized and is reflected in all process and systems in the organization.
4. Technology-enabled: ICT is leveraged and used well.
5. Focus on results: the results of knowledge work are monitored and measured.

The COVID-19 pandemic has allowed us to take full advantage of our ICT infrastructure. We must find a way not to leave this behind in 2023 when we're back to a more familiar time.

The Knowledge Management Action Plan 2021–2025 envisions continuous process improvements, and ADB transitioning from a knowledge bank ("know what") to a solution bank ("know how"). Rather than focusing on the number of knowledge products and services produced, it calls for measuring the impact of knowledge solutions applied to complex problems across DMCs. The process of managing knowledge is shifting, from collecting and capturing knowledge, to co-creating and curating knowledge solutions across ADB, with partners, and advancing innovation through iterative processes. In parallel with this, knowledge silos and repositories will be replaced with knowledge solution networks.

The new action plan supports a theory of change, outlining how ADB can "become a leading and trusted provider of knowledge solutions and contribute to better-informed policies, innovative programs and projects, and operations in DMCs." The theory of change outlines a set of causal relationships that determine how a set of actions will bring about the most desired outcomes for intended beneficiaries and the theory anchors actions on people, processes, and relationships.

Its expected outputs are as follows:

1. People and culture incentivized to create and promote knowledge solutions (including through a value-based culture transformation initiative, talent management, recruitment and learning programs).
2. Processes and systems streamlined for client-oriented knowledge creation, flow and use such as stronger country knowledge programming, collaborating with the resident mission, and implementing an ADB Digital Agenda.
3. Relationships built and nurtured across departments within ADB and with knowledge partners in DMCs and beyond, including through ADB partnership tools and modalities for engaging knowledge partners.

Cross-departmental initiatives include an innovation framework; a digital agenda; a CPS reform and review action plan; a review of resident mission operations; leadership, staff learning, skills and talent development programs; and a culture transformation initiative.

The future of knowledge management will rely on innovation, but also on repurposing existing knowledge from across sectors, themes, countries, and regions. To adapt to local realities, knowledge solutions have to be easily retrievable where and when they are needed, and that relies on modern ICT infrastructure embedded into a learning organization. ADB's agility in terms of producing knowledge solutions and influence critical reforms to address current socioeconomic problems will face its biggest task yet, as DMCs begin their process of recovery from the COVID-19 pandemic.

The ADB Institute: Vision, Milestones, and Achievements

The creation of a specialized research and training institution that would help advance ADB's core development objectives in Asia and the Pacific came about in May 1996. At the 29th Annual Meeting of the Board of Governors, it was proposed that this new institute could broaden the reach of ADB's training efforts and foster evidence-based policy solutions. As ADB's think tank, the institute was expected to approach emerging issues and debates in an innovative and forward-thinking way, complementing the work of the bank's economic research and knowledge departments.

Since then, ADBI has provided high-quality and timely research, capacity building, and outreach support for sustainable and inclusive development in Asia and the Pacific. ADBI has done so by offering policy makers and other stakeholders research for more effectively pursuing strategic development priorities, building implementation capabilities through training programs and policy forums, and promoting awareness and uptake of ADBI solutions. ADBI has also established far-reaching partnerships with a diverse range of think tanks, universities, research institutes, government agencies, and international organizations, amplifying its project scope and impact.

ADBI continues to strengthen its role as a thought leader through key global and regional think tank networks. This includes active participation in the Think20, the think tank engagement group of the Group of 20 (G20), which ADBI chaired in 2019 as part of Japan's G20 presidency. ADBI also presents an Asia and Pacific perspective in think tank forums

under the University of Pennsylvania's Think Tanks and Civil Societies Program and Global Solutions Initiative, while exploring new opportunities to provide guidance and support for think tanks across the region to further common sustainable development objectives.

In recognition of its work, ADBI was ranked by its peers as the top government affiliated think tank worldwide for a second consecutive year in 2020 and 24th in the overall think tank ranking in the *Go To Think Tank Index Report*.[20] Today, COVID-19 pandemic recovery imperatives and Sustainable Development Goals (SDGs) are driving ADBI to build on this progress. It will continue to do so by leveraging its nimbleness and flexibility, prioritizing a policy-oriented and demand-driven approach, and harnessing digital tools. It will take new and dynamic approaches to research, capacity building, and outreach; and the strong but fast-changing nature of demand for policy knowledge among economies in Asia and the Pacific, in line with "One ADB" and Strategy 2030.

---

[20]   McGann, James G., 2021. *2020 Global Go to Think Tank Index Report*. TTCSP Global Go to Think Tank Index Reports. 18.

Knowledge Partnerships

Knowledge partnerships play an integral role in ADBI's research activities. Think tank researchers, academics, policy makers from regional members and beyond, and staff of ADB and other international institutions act as trusted partners in ongoing research and knowledge sharing. ADBI maintains ongoing relations with various institutions through memoranda of understanding and similar relationships, including the CAREC Institute, Singapore National University, and Stanford University. ADBI also promotes knowledge sharing through its visiting researcher program, adjunct lecturing at local universities, and interviewee and commentator services to mass media outlets.

Most recently, ADBI teamed up with the Cambridge Centre for Alternative Finance of Cambridge University to set up a dedicated research unit in Singapore to cover financial technology developments in the region. ADBI has recruited a number of prominent scholars to be on the editorial board of its newly established ADBI Press book series on sustainable development in Asia and the Pacific. During its leadership of the Japan Think20 process in 2019, ADBI was able to establish new relationships with researchers in various regions outside Asia.

ADBI also leverages its knowledge partnerships for capacity building and training activities. This is done through annual policy dialogues on prominent themes in Asia where high-level officials meet to share ideas; and course-based training, which also benefits from expertise that participating officials bring.

One ADB

ADBI takes a "One ADB" approach, working closely with ADB counterparts and knowledge departments to avoid duplication of effort. It pools research in shared repositories and platforms, such as the in-house portal k-Nexus or the publicly searchable Think-Asia repository. ADBI is an active partner in ADB's KMAP, as well as the country knowledge plans, to ensure alignment with country knowledge needs.

Looking Ahead

ADBI has become a vital incubation space for public policy professionals, with excellent secondees from DMC governments and ADB, researchers from universities, and other experts. It provides them with ample opportunities for cross-fertilization of ideas and views, and with a variety of new experiences before they return to their home organizations or join other institutions. ADBI has faced some challenges, such as its small size relative to other outstanding think tanks and its short-term employment practice, which have made it difficult for it to cover a wide range of issues and conduct deep and hence time-consuming studies. These disadvantages notwithstanding, ADBI has produced a considerable amount of high-quality knowledge.

The COVID-19 pandemic has highlighted the need for rapid flows of knowledge. It has also shown how existing technology allows patterns and knowledge to be extracted quickly from large amounts of data. Future crises—linked to climate change, pandemics, weak financial structures, for example—will likely trigger significant demand for quick knowledge solutions and rapid dissemination. Innovation in the use of data and technology will fuel people's expectations, leading to even stronger demand.

The implication for think tanks is that even large quantities of high-quality knowledge products made by the biggest think tanks in the world will be regarded as a tiny contribution, compared with the huge increase in demand. In the future, rather than focusing on quantity and quality of knowledge products, it will become more important for think tanks to direct or shape rapid flows of knowledge, and thus, its relatively small size and short-term employment practice might no longer put ADBI at a disadvantage.

A potential advantage of ADBI is that governments, think tanks, and universities in the region consider ADBI as a natural focal point of regional cooperation. In the future, ADBI will make full use of digital technology to engage in regional cooperation across Asia and the Pacific. It will also create regional hubs of international cooperation and make greater intellectual contributions to solving shared policy issues across ADB's DMCs.

Challenges, Breakthroughs, Impact: Knowledge Solutions

AGRICULTURE AND FOOD SECURITY

EDUCATION

ENERGY

ENVIRONMENT

FINANCE

As ADB's knowledge management has evolved, across the entire organization project teams have been empowered to put knowledge solutions at the center of their work with DMCs. The case studies that follow showcase just some of the many successes in knowledge management over the years and highlight ADB's evolving role as a key source of advice, information, and intelligence.

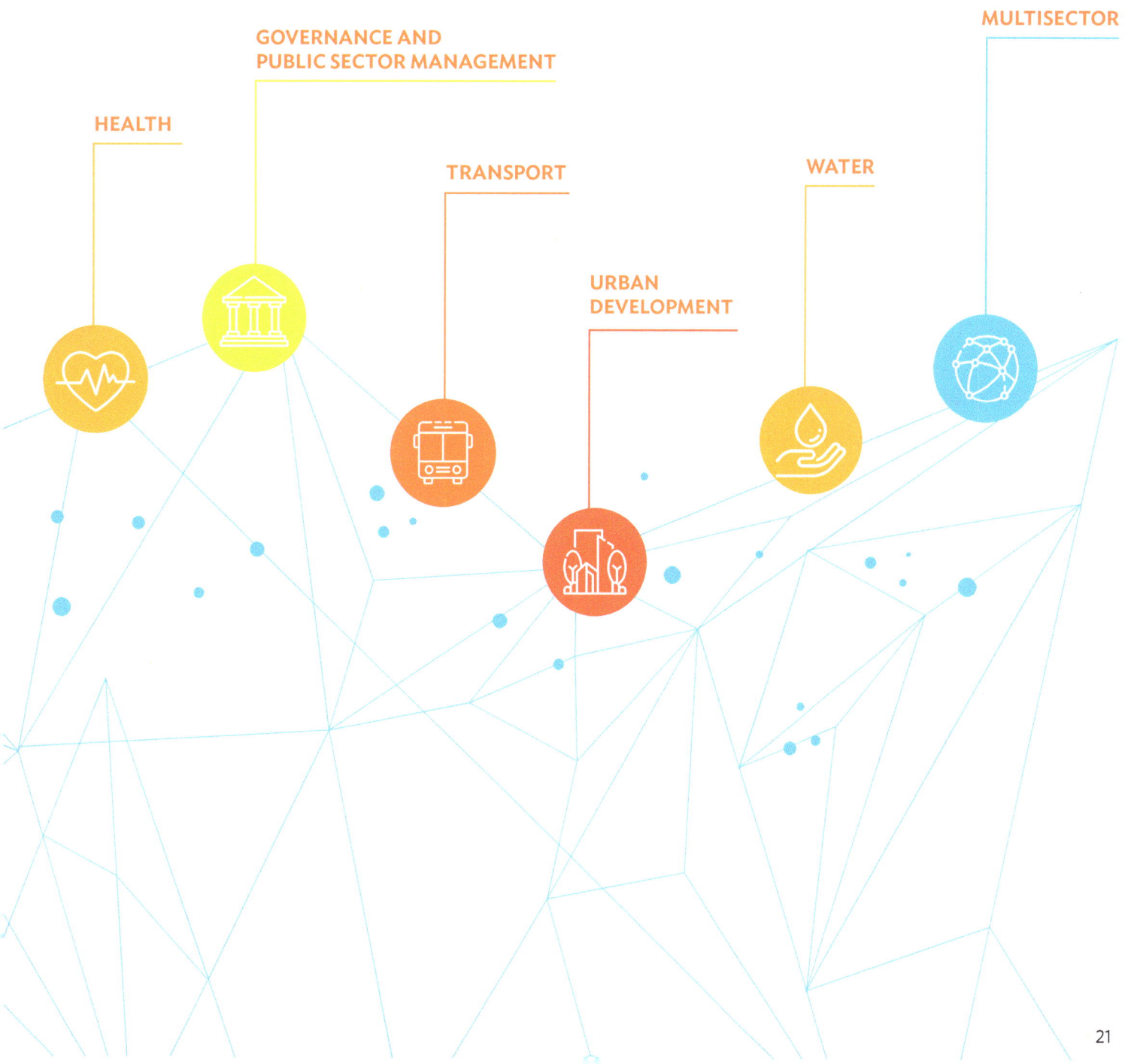

HEALTH

GOVERNANCE AND
PUBLIC SECTOR MANAGEMENT

TRANSPORT

URBAN
DEVELOPMENT

WATER

MULTISECTOR

Improved Food Security in the Lao People's Democratic Republic

Project Name:	Northern Rural Infrastructure Development Sector Project
Region/Country:	Southeast Asia/Lao People's Democratic Republic
Sector and Themes:	Agriculture and Food Security
Year:	2011–Present
Team Leader (current):	Khamtanh Chanthy

The project highlights the importance of complementary capacity building initiatives for national, provincial, and district agencies to enable the creation of a sector development approach.

Improved irrigation facilities and agriculture infrastructure can help food security for the Lao People's Democratic Republic.

Development challenge

Less than 10% of the land in the Lao People's Democratic Republic (Lao PDR) was classified as arable, with only about one-fifth irrigated. Mountainous terrain, drought, and lack of infrastructure restricted arable land and the farming seasons, often threatening the year's food crop.

Solution

Year-round crop growing through improved irrigation facilities and agriculture infrastructure can help ensure food security for the Lao PDR. ADB is helping the country improve agriculture infrastructure in the northern regions to boost farm yields and income, through improved irrigation systems and rural access roads. The project has rehabilitated and upgraded rural access roads from the command irrigation areas to villages. A first phase financed through the Asian Development Fund (ADF), the Northern Rural

Infrastructure Development Sector Project, targeted 26 gravity-fed irrigation schemes to improve water supply in arid farmland. Additional ADF grants of $35.6 million targeted funding for 22 additional irrigation systems and new farm access roads.

Knowledge products and services delivered

The project has supported improved monitoring and evaluation, and the creation of water user groups, and farmer production groups for improved management of agriculture land, for farmers' more bargaining power to negotiate with buyers.
The project helped train water user groups and farmer production groups to better manage the upgraded and newly created infrastructure. It has supported subproject beneficiaries and producer groups to coordinate supplies of agricultural products to markets and processors and contracted

agricultural production with price incentives based on quality and introduced initiatives to secure land tenure and access to land for sedentary agricultural production. Land rezoning helped protect the integrity of watersheds and reservoirs. Institutional capacity building was also provided for national and subnational agencies toward a sector development approach.

These helped to improve agricultural productivity, diversify crops, and commercialize the low-performing agriculture sector in the northern region. There are 33 ongoing training programs in technical, social, and geographic information systems, project monitoring and evaluation, operation and maintenance, value chain development, and financial management. These programs will train almost 3,000 trainees (29% women). Some 60 water user groups and village road maintenance committees were established and registered for all the 22 subprojects.

The water user groups have 276 members, of which 116 (42%) are women, and the village road maintenance committees have 55 members (33% women). Fourteen farmer production groups were established at 12 subprojects. They have implemented contract farming with local and Chinese investors to sell their commercialized agriculture production to Chinese border markets.

Impact and results

The project supported increased agricultural productivity in the four northern provinces of Bokeo, Luang Namtha, Oudomxay, and Phongsaly. With gravity irrigation, most of the farmers have focused on planting commercialized agriculture products with high market demand, where they can earn a more stable income. The project has also improved irrigation systems and strengthened food security.

Ongoing training programs for 3,000 male and female trainees will help improve agricultural productivity.

Lessons for replication

The project highlights the importance of complementary capacity building initiatives for national, provincial, and district agencies for a sector development approach. Study tours enabled project participants to visit and exchange lessons with others, learn good practice, build networks, and exchange technical experience.

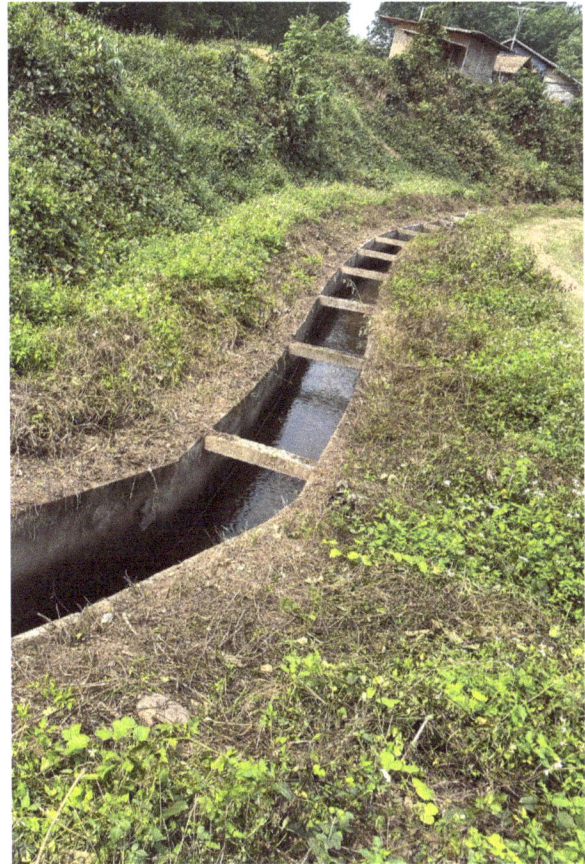

The project has improved irrigation systems and strengthened food security.

Hashtags:
#LaoPDR, #Agriculture, #Transport, #FoodSecurity, #Training, #HelpToFarmers

Find out more:
• https://bit.ly/3DHAYgh

Enhancing the Potential of Wholesale Markets through Training on Market Infrastructure and Agriculture Value Chains in Spain

Project Name:	Training on Market Infrastructure and Agriculture Value Chains: The Potential of Wholesale Markets, 24–28 July 2017 and 24–28 June 2019, Spain
Region/Country:	Regional/Indonesia, Kazakhstan, Nepal, Pakistan, Philippines, Uzbekistan, and Viet Nam
Sector and Themes:	Agriculture and Food Security
Year:	2016–Present
Project Leader:	Md. Abul Basher

Having watched during these days how Mercasa has been solving issues and challenges throughout its history, it's a very good example for us of what needs to be done in our country to make an efficient system of food distribution.
—Kazakhstan Study Tour Participant

Through training, the project helped disseminate best practices in agricultural market infrastructure and value chains.

Development challenge

Over a billion people in Asia still suffer from food insecurity, threatening to reverse progress to date in ending hunger and malnutrition. This progress has been slow due to the complex nature of food security, which is affected by multiple factors, including climate change, natural resource depletion, rapid urbanization, competing use of agricultural resources by other sectors, and aging populations. The problem is aggravated by post-harvest losses— a failure to bring the food from field to market.

In ADB's DMCs, poorly planned and dispersed nature of agri-supply chains are easily disrupted by crises like the COVID-19 pandemic, further threatening food security. Weak agriculture value chains also make it difficult for authorities to ensure the safety of agricultural produce. Strengthening agricultural market infrastructure and value chains can play a huge role in supplying reliable, fresh, and safe food to growing urban populations, and to tackling hunger and nutrition insecurities.

Solution

The project disseminated best practices in operation of these markets that could then be implemented in DMCs. For selected DMCs, the project assessed the legal and institutional environment for supporting wholesale markets and developed effective custom-tailored models. ADB developed the capacity of DMC government officials through training programs and study tours in managing wholesale markets.

Knowledge products and services delivered

In 2017, ADB organized a training program and study tour in Spain for 12 government officials from Kazakhstan, Nepal, Uzbekistan, and Viet Nam and relevant ADB staff. In 2019, two similar programs were organized for officials from Indonesia, Pakistan, and the Philippines to visit Spain and France.

Impact and results

The project imparted knowledge and skills on design, setup, and operations of wholesale markets

to both ADB staff and government officials from seven DMCs. Best practices learned through physical visits to European wholesale markets were shared, leading to several DMCs expressing interest for setting up wholesale markets. In Bangladesh, Nepal, Pakistan, and Viet Nam, the project also assessed the potential for setting up and improving wholesale markets. Wholesale market projects were designed in Kazakhstan and Uzbekistan. Currently, the Government of Pakistan is working to develop a wholesale market in Lahore with support from ADB. Knowledge gained in this project also spilled over within ADB, resulting in pipeline projects in India.

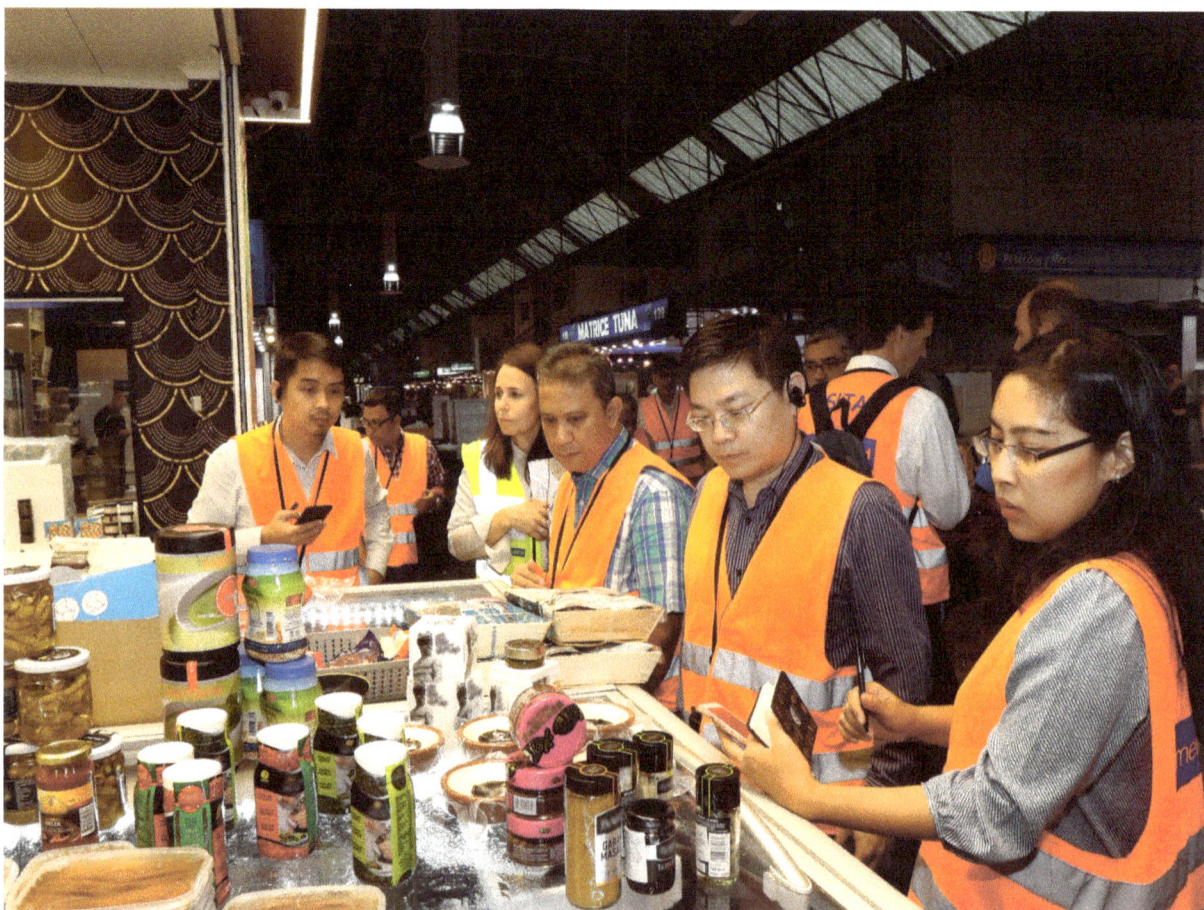

ADB staff and government officials from seven developing member countries learned about the design, setup, and operations of wholesale markets.

Former ADB Vice-President Diwakar Gupta and former ADB Chief of Rural Development and Food Security (Agriculture) Thematic Group Akmal Siddiq.

Lessons for replication

The project highlights the importance of practical, context-oriented programmatic knowledge sharing as a solution to disseminate best practices in managing wholesale markets. The opportunity for peer knowledge exchanges, and connecting government officials, farmers, producers' cooperatives, and management in Spain increased interest among other DMCs wholesale markets to improve their agriculture value chains as a solution to hunger and malnutrition.

> "
> *With support from ADB, Uzbekistan will start working in the conceptualization of three wholesale markets. The support of ADB for the implementation market research in Tashkent, Samarkand, and Fergana Valley will surely be a very important milestone.*
>
> **—Uzbekistan Study Tour Participant**

Hashtags:
#Agriculture, #AgricultureMarkets, #WholesaleMarkets, #StudyTours #CapacityBuilding, #Regional

Find out more:
- https://bit.ly/3BLzAIT
- https://bit.ly/3AJi9Yb
- https://bit.ly/3AMsHFY
- https://bit.ly/3FQXNQs

Promoting Prosperity and Equality in Indonesia and Timor-Leste

Project Name: Enhanced Cooperation and Integration between Indonesia and Timor-Leste: Scoping Study

Region/Country: Southeast Asia/Indonesia and Timor-Leste

Sector and Themes: Agriculture and Food Security

Year: 2017–Present

Project Leader: Anna Fink

> *Supporting livelihoods in lagging border areas is critical to tackling inequality and ensuring our region's growing prosperity is shared by all.*
> **—Takehiko Nakao, Former President, ADB**

ADB President Takehiko Nakao, Indonesia's Minister of Finance Sri Mulyani Indrawati (left), and Timor-Leste's Minister (Acting) of Finance Sara Lobo Brites (right) at the signing of the memorandum of understanding in Nadi, Fiji in May 2019.

Development challenge

Enhancing regional cooperation between markets in Asia and the Pacific is a critical driver for spurring economic growth and reducing inequality. The Trans-Pacific Partnership and the Regional Comprehensive Economic Partnership are both stellar examples of cooperation and integration in the region.

In 2017, Indonesia requested support from ADB in tackling spatial inequality and poverty in the nation's second-poorest province, Nusa Tenggara Timur. Meanwhile, Timor-Leste required assistance on its Strategic Development Plan goals for economic growth and diversification, and specifically on its application for membership to the Association of Southeast Asian Nations (ASEAN).

Both governments requested assistance to explore avenues for cross-border cooperation.

Solution

ADB's Regional Cooperation and Integration (RCI) Thematic Group led the scoping study with assistance from the Pacific Department and Southeast Asia Department (SERD). The RCI group worked with the Fiscal Policy Agency in Indonesia and the Fiscal Policy Commission in Timor-Leste to consult with more than 250 individuals in government, the private sector, and civil society in both countries. Previous studies conducted in Timor-Leste under the Pacific Department's Trade and Transport Facilitation in the Pacific and other studies conducted by SERD on cross-border cooperation between Indonesia and Malaysia were used. Funding from the study included cofinancing from Australia and the United Kingdom.

Knowledge products and services delivered

ADB published *Enhanced Cooperation and Integration between Indonesia and Timor-Leste: Scoping Study,* which identified areas of cooperation as well as barriers between Indonesia and Timor-Leste. It explored opportunities that could arise from establishing a border economic zone linked to an economic corridor such as livestock trade and cross-border tourism. Trade and transport facilitation were identified as essential enablers.

Impact and results

The recommendations of the scoping study were used to draft a memorandum of understanding (MOU) between ADB, Indonesia, and Timor-Leste

in May 2019. Both countries pledged to reduce barriers to cross-border land and air transportation and harmonize procedures at border crossing points. It also sought to reduce animal health barriers to livestock trade and bolster tourism promotion in Nusa Tenggara Timur and Timor-Leste through joint marketing. ADB granted $1 million (TA 9767) to support implementation of the MOU.

Based on agreements in the MOU, the Government of Timor-Leste removed visa fees for Indonesian tourists entering Timor-Leste. A Timor-Leste immigration officer at Mota'ain border post between Indonesia and Timor-Leste reported that visitors increased from 300 to 400 per day. The TA supported discussions among the governments on the text of an MOU for cross-border movement of buses and coaches, which will remove barriers to seamless transport connectivity.

Delegations from the High-Level Dialogue between Indonesia and Timor-Leste wrapped up the scoping study on cross-border cooperation in a meeting held in Bali, Indonesia in March 2019.

Lessons for replication

The scoping study provides critical insights on how to identify avenues and sectors for cooperation and integration between two countries and implement the same. ADB's RCI thematic group can use this study for guidance on key issues affecting the future of regional cooperation in the Asia and Pacific region.

Consultations were conducted in Indonesia and Timor-Leste to refine the priority actions under the memorandum of understanding. In the photo is ADB Country Director for Timor-Leste Resident Mission Sunil Mitra giving remarks in a consultation meeting held in 2019.

> *Timor-Leste has made significant strides since independence but if this is to continue, we must integrate more closely into ASEAN and the world economy as well as diversify our economy. Reducing barriers to trade and cooperation with our closest neighbors is an essential step in achieving this goal.*
>
> **—Sara Lobo Brites, Timor-Leste Acting Minister of Finance**

Hashtags:

#SoutheastAsia, #Indonesia, #TimorLeste, #RegionalCooperation, #MOU, #Trade, #Logistics

Find out more:
- https://bit.ly/3AFXyE9
- https://bit.ly/3aEF1xG
- https://bit.ly/3j3zx3Z
- https://bit.ly/3DJihc4
- https://bit.ly/3j3zx3Z

Reforming Curriculum Design and Pedagogy for Improved Learning in Uzbekistan

Project Name:	Basic Education Textbook Development Project
Region/Country:	Central and West Asia/Uzbekistan
Sector and Themes:	Education
Year:	1998–2004
Project Leaders:	Marc Cohen and Zulfia Karimova

The project also introduced new thinking and practices, thus enhancing capacities within the Ministry of Public Education.

Development challenge

Basic education in Uzbekistan was underfunded after its independence in 1991 as the country was shifting to a market economy. Lacking essential inputs and operating within the old outdated system of education, the quality, relevance, and access to basic education became major concerns for the government. Textbooks were outdated and unaffordable. This impacted the morale of educators and students, and significantly reduced learning.

In 1995, the government started to implement a change in the medium of instruction from Uzbek Cyrillic to Latin script, requiring a comprehensive rewriting and reprinting of textbooks. Thus, improving education quality by providing textbooks that are better designed, more affordable, and more durable—as the textbooks are rented out—became a priority for the education sector. At the same time, during this time, the government restructured and extended compulsory education to 12 years, introduced state education standards, and abolished provision of free textbooks by the state.

Solution

Uzbekistan and ADB became partners in 1995, and one of the first projects was to produce a large quantity of good quality textbooks with modern content. The Basic Education Textbook Development Project (BETDP), approved in December 1997, comprised two components: a development finance institution loan of $20 million for publishers and printers for upgrading equipment and procuring high-quality paper and cover board;

The project helped produce 49,000 visual aids, more than 60 million textbooks in six different languages, and 2 million teachers' guides for basic education.

and a project loan of $20 million for other project components, including capacity building, and purchase of selected textbooks.

Knowledge products and services delivered

The project enabled publishing of new textbooks and built the capacity of teachers. It supported publishing of more than 60 million textbooks in 6 different languages, 2 million teachers' guides, and 49,000 visual aids. The capacity of the Ministry of Public Education and teachers were built through TA that included training on the new pedagogy and learning curriculum.

Impact and results

The introduction of an innovative textbook rental scheme allowed parents to pay a fraction of textbook purchase price as rental fees. This made the supply more sustainable, as fees collected are designated for buying replacement copies of textbooks. The program also helped enhance skills and capacities through the newly developed curriculum, improved pedagogical and methodical quality of textbooks and learning material, and guides for teachers. Enhanced capacities within the Ministry of Public Education has continued to benefit ADB operations in basic education and contributed to cumulative progress in education sector reforms. To augment the success of the BETDP, ADB approved the Second Textbook Development Project (Loan 2093) that enabled the pilot textbook rental scheme to become part of the wider education system, benefiting more than 4.5 million school children annually. The project helped extend textbook rental coverage to all grades and all basic education schools. It also institutionalized the textbook rental scheme and its funding mechanism through the Special Republican Book Fund Foundation to ensure sustainable provision of affordable textbooks.

Children's education improved vastly through a newly developed curriculum, improved quality of textbooks and learning materials, and teacher's guides.

Lessons for replication

The textbook rental scheme made textbooks easily available and affordable for all. Lessons also apply through improved pedagogy and teaching material. The BETDP offers valuable lessons for improved impact monitoring in future projects.

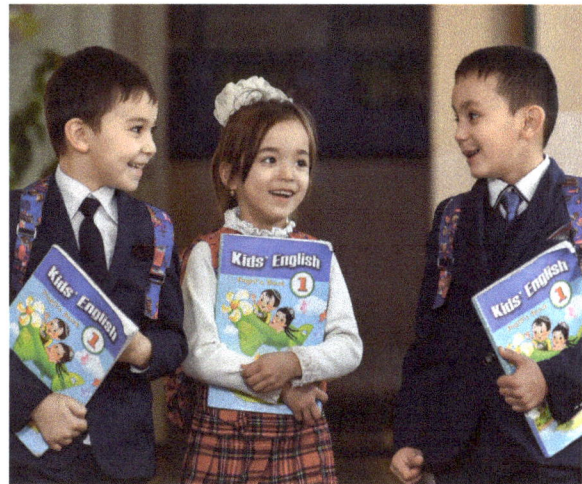

Parents were able to save through the use of an innovative textbook rental scheme developed under the project.

Hashtags:

#ReadMore, #Education, #EducationalReforms, #Uzbekistan, #Textbooks, #Learning

Find out more:

- https://bit.ly/3DH0xOz
- https://bit.ly/3lFc7nk
- https://bit.ly/3j3t49i
- https://bit.ly/3lFxchq

Protecting Schools in Armenia from Earthquakes

Project Name:	Seismic Safety Improvement Program
Country:	Armenia
Sector and Themes:	Education
Year:	2016–Present
Project Leader:	Gohar Mousaelyan

The newly built schools have created a unique environment that will contribute to the change in the worldview of the students, contributing to their development.

—Artur Soghomonyan, executive director, Armenian Development Territorial Fund

Development challenge

Since the massive Spitak earthquake in 1988, national authorities in Armenia have taken numerous steps to develop emergency management and response systems and to improve building design and construction. To become earthquake resilient, approximately 1,000 of the country's 1,400 schools required strengthening and reconstruction work, at an estimated cost of $1.2 billion.

ADB is supporting ongoing efforts of the Government of Armenia to rebuild and strengthen school buildings to higher earthquake-resistant standards and to further develop the government's capacity, ownership, and initiative in the management of earthquake risks.

Solution

ADB provided $89.3 million in assistance to help Armenia build earthquake-resilient schools and scale up its capacity for responding to natural disasters. The program focuses on the four priorities in the Sendai Framework for Disaster Risk Reduction, 2015–2030: understanding disaster risk; strengthening disaster risk governance to manage disaster risk; investing in disaster risk reduction for resilience; and enhancing disaster preparedness for effective response, and rebuilding better in recovery, rehabilitation, and reconstruction. The program is improving school seismic safety to reduce casualties and damage in schools during earthquakes and enabling better use of school buildings as shelters for

The program is improving school seismic safety to reduce casualties and damage in schools during earthquakes.

the general public and as focal points for emergency response after earthquakes. Thus, the program has also supported the implementation of the Armenia National Disaster Risk Management Strategy.

Knowledge products and services delivered

The capacity building component included improving the capacity of approximately 60 engineers, construction managers, and workers in seismic strengthening construction technology, knowledge, techniques, and skills. The program also updated and harmonized national building codes with international standards for seismic safety. These initiatives helped the government to improve its systems and enhance its already strong ownership, invest in school seismic strengthening and renovation using its own systems,

and develop a platform for implementing investment projects funded by development partners.

Impact and results

The project will benefit approximately 58,700 students, teachers, and other staff, as well as more than 87,000 residents living near the target schools, who will have access to improved temporary shelters during earthquakes. ADB's loan and grant will support improvements to at least 46 priority schools. It will also help the target schools develop disaster preparedness and response plans, with earthquake

The program updated and harmonized national building codes with international standards for seismic safety.

The program helped enable better use of school buildings as shelters for the public and as focal points for emergency response after earthquakes.

awareness campaigns to be carried out in neighborhood communities for each school.

Lessons for replication

The school survey examined many previously unknown attempted activities: the costs of conducting a survey of building vulnerability, the technical expertise required for this type of survey, and the costs involved in strengthening existing vulnerable buildings. These factors can be considered if this project gets implemented in another country.

> *The completed schools are not only earthquake resistant but also are inclusive, providing access for persons with disabilities, and they have comfortable gymnasiums, canteens, laboratories, and libraries. The program has given impetus to revise the approach to school design to comply with 21st century educational standards.*
> **—Gohar Mousaelyan, project officer, ADB**

Hashtags:
#Armenia, #Earthquake, #NaturalDisaster, #Education, #EarthquakeRelief, #ADB

Find out more:
- https://bit.ly/3AGQIUw
- https://bit.ly/3mYrS82
- https://bit.ly/3p05gXD

Bridging the Education–Employment Gap in Sri Lanka

Project Name: Education Sector Development Program

Region/Country: South Asia/Sri Lanka

Sector and Themes: Education

Year: 2013–2019

Project Leader: Herathbanda Jayasundara

> *My engagement with IT opened up more opportunities for me, and I could enhance my skills by using new knowledge.*
>
> **—Kavindi Madushika, graduate, Rambuka Maha Vidyalaya High School, Pothupitiya**

Development challenge

In the 1960s, Sri Lanka was mostly rural with high rates of poverty and low rates of education and literacy. The challenge was to bridge the gap between education and employability. It was important to produce graduates with science and technology skills who would be sought after by employers and encourage participation from female students in this sector.

Solution

To help Sri Lanka make the transition from a labor market to a knowledge economy, ADB approved the Education Sector Development Program in 2013. This was the first ever results-based loan (RBL) that targeted upgrading school classrooms and laboratories and improving teacher training in science and technology. The loan had clearly defined indicators—number of improved schools and trained teachers—that ensured the loan was targeted to achieve maximum benefit.

This first ever results-based loan helped upgrade school classrooms and laboratories and improved teacher training in science and technology.

Knowledge products and services delivered

The project introduced several initiatives to improve the quality of training in science and technology. In particular, the project introduced technology courses that allowed secondary school graduates to move more easily into vocational courses, thus supporting their future employability. It also upgraded 255 rural secondary schools to offer science and commerce streams for the General Certificate of Education (GCE) Advanced Level with required teacher training and capacity development of school management.

Impact and results

This was the first ever successful RBL. It helped educators and school administrators improve the financing, management, and planning at schools. The technology stream opened the education system by showing students a wider range of opportunities and has aligned schools more closely to the labor market. Skills and competencies were developed in teachers through the teacher training programs. Upgraded secondary schools provided 5,381 GCE Advanced Level students with the opportunity to study science when they might not have done otherwise. The enrollment numbers

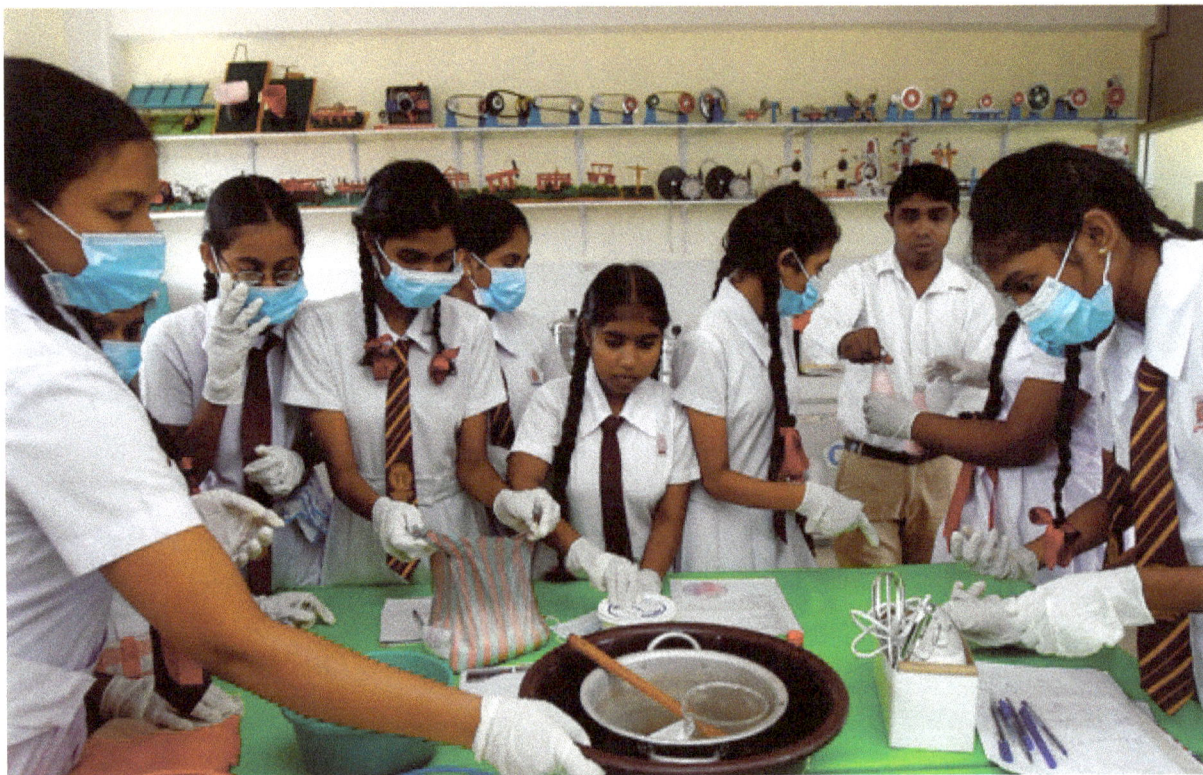

The project introduced technology courses that supported the future employability of secondary school graduates.

increased, and it is hoped that with time the new GCE Advanced Level science schools will become better established and quality of education will improve.

Lessons for replication

An RBL, if designed appropriately, can support improving the classrooms, training the teachers in science and technology, introducing new and interesting vocational technology courses, and ensuring the effective use of funds to produce the right results. However, the monitoring framework for such loans should be kept simple, so that the indicators are monitored regularly and with ease, and documents streamlined for consistency.

Through the project, enrollment numbers increased.

> *I wanted to try engineering technology, even though the majority who chose the course were males. I like that subject a lot. If males can, why can't we?*
> **—Female student from Rajarata University**

Hashtags:
#SouthAsia, #Books, #Science, #Technology, #SriLanka, #Loan

Find out more:
- https://bit.ly/3AGQIUw
- https://bit.ly/3p4TV8M

Technical and Vocational Assistance in Timor-Leste for Supporting Development

Project Name: Mid-Level Skills Training Project

Country: Timor-Leste

Sector and Themes: Education

Year: 2012–2018

Project Leader: Ninebeth Carandang

> *People in Manatuto think that women can't work in construction. But now men and women have the same rights to do the same things! I am looking forward to graduating from this course. I want to show my certificate to women from the districts, which will prove that women can do it too.*
>
> **—Diolinda Ximenes, trainee, Tibar Training Center**

Development challenge

Timor-Leste is Asia's youngest country. It has moved past the strife of recent years and is undertaking the difficult work of building a strong, resilient economy that benefits all. The development of a skilled workforce is much needed for Timor-Leste's rapidly expanding economy.

Solution

ADB supported the development of a skilled workforce for Timor-Leste's rapidly expanding economy. It used extensive regional experience in technical and vocational education and training (TVET) to help the government reduce mid-level skills shortages. The Mid-Level Skills Training

Project, approved in 2012, enhanced the capacities of the accredited construction and automotive training providers in the country by introducing and implementing mid-level skills training in construction and automotive trades.

The project built on existing training programs and facilities. By filling skills gaps in the current system of TVET, the project supported the government to develop a skilled workforce and improve employment opportunities for men and women in Timor-Leste. The project ensured that at least one in five of the trainees is female, and encouraged female participation with scholarships, separate amenities, and gender awareness training.

At least one in five of the trainees under the project is female, and female participation is encouraged through scholarships, separate amenities, and gender awareness training.

The project supported seven training centers, and between 2012 and 2018, 2,445 people were trained, including 618 women.

Knowledge products and services delivered

The project focused on key elements such as development of competency-based training standards and improving the quality of teaching staff, facilitating the role of the private sector, and strengthening the labor market information system to build demand-driven skills training relevant and responsive to the needs of the expanding economy of Timor-Leste.

The project harmonized and built on the assistance provided by existing development partners in the TVET sector, including the Australian Agency for International Development, the International Labour Organization, the European Commission, the Government of Brazil, and the Spanish International Cooperation.

Impact and results

With 25% of trainees being female, the project exceeded its female participation target—and trained and facilitated employment for the country's first female mechanics. By late 2015, the project had trained 47 teachers from 5 construction-training centers, with diploma programs in mechanical, civil, and engineering conducted by the State Polytechnic of Malang, Indonesia. All training was carried out in Timor-Leste instead of overseas. Construction of Tibar Dormitory was completed. The project supported seven training centers, and between 2012 and 2018, 2,445 people were trained, including 618 women. Mid-level trainees also received on-the-job practical skills provided through industry partnerships.

Lessons for replication

The project highlights the hybrid model of classroom and on-the-job experience. Industry partnerships help in the delivery of on-the-job technical and practical skills through accredited training programs. It emphasizes the relevance of a labor market information system that supports demand-driven skills training. It showcases how harmonized efforts by building upon existing TVET programs delivered by the other development partners contribute to a project's success.

> *I want this training center to continue achieving quality in its training. This will give faith to young people that the training prepares them with professional knowledge and skills so that they can compete in the job market, create their own work, and make an income for them, their families and their communities.*
>
> **—Simão Barreto, director, Tibar Training Center**

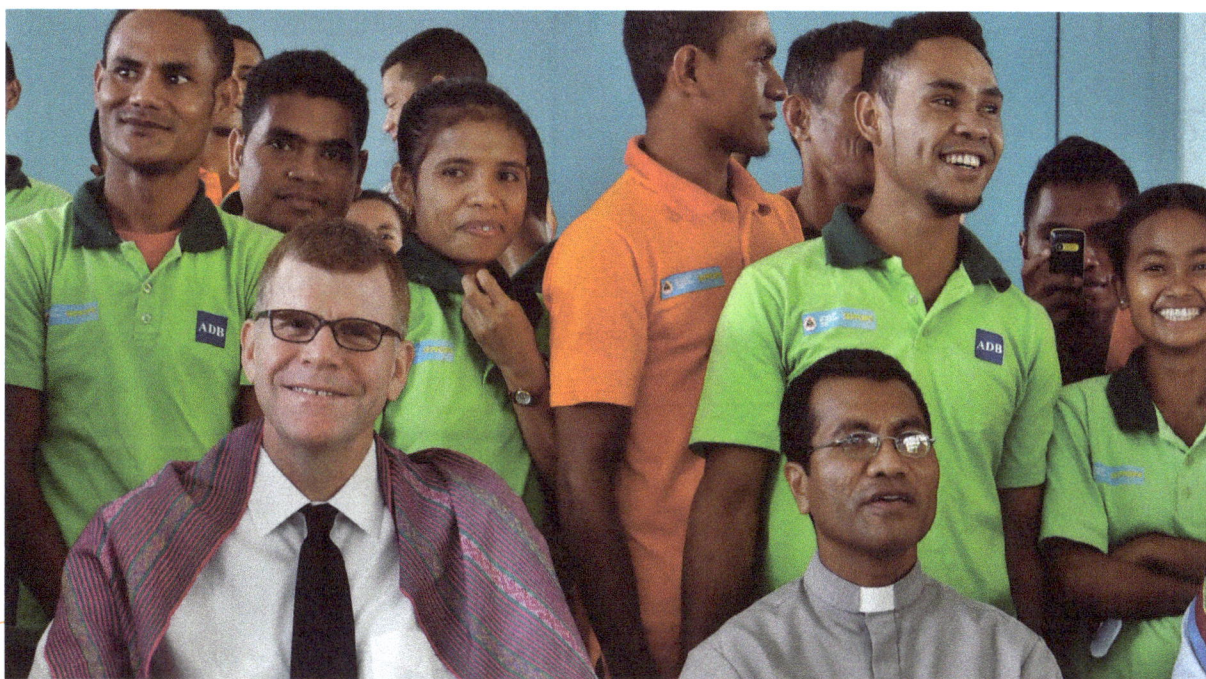

Former ADB Vice-President Stephen Groff with the project's graduates.

Hashtags:
#TimorLeste, #Education, #Training, #VocationalTraining, #TechnicalTraining

Find out more:
- https://bit.ly/3j5xSLn
- https://bit.ly/3AGQIUw

Earthquake Rehabilitation and Reconstruction of Schools in Nepal

Project Name:	Earthquake Emergency Assistance Project (TA 8910: Developing Earthquake-Resilient Type Designs of Remote Schools Using Locally Available Materials)
Region/Country:	South Asia/Nepal
Sector and Themes:	Education
Year:	2015–2019
Project Leader:	Naresh Giri

We knew we had to build the permanent structures quickly to retain the students as well as get back to the pre-earthquake enrollment numbers.

—Lokendra Dhakal, headmaster, Sanjiwani Secondary School, Nepal

Development challenge

The magnitude 7.8 earthquake that struck Nepal on 25 April 2015 resulted in colossal damage. More than 7,500 school buildings are still being reconstructed in accordance with the build–back–better (BBB) approach, which uses modern construction materials such as cement and steel. However, a significant part of the earthquake-affected areas is in highly rugged terrain and inaccessible by road. This triggered a need for evidence-based earthquake-resistance design of school buildings in remote areas of Nepal.

Solution

ADB worked with the National Reconstruction Authority to strengthen the government's BBB and resilience programs, incorporating lessons from recent disasters in other Asian countries. This entailed rehabilitation or reconstruction of school buildings, improved road access, and training to ensure proper monitoring of new infrastructure, as well as future school building design, to ensure disaster resilience.

The school buildings were designed using locally available materials and skills, and minimal use of imported materials. ADB's TA provided in-depth research to demonstrate load-bearing, masonry-type school buildings were developed using stone and mud, which have been approved by the Ministry of Urban Development.

ADB worked with the National Reconstruction Authority to strengthen the government's build–back–better and resilience programs, which entailed rehabilitation or reconstruction of school buildings, among others.

Knowledge products and services delivered

A special purpose vehicle was set up by the government to manage the reconstruction programs with high efficiency through focused, streamlined, and flexible decision making in budgetary, implementation, and monitoring and evaluation processes. ADB helped build the capacities of executing and implementing agencies on procurement, contract management, quality control, and disbursement for education facilities. Partnerships with sector agencies were renewed and strengthened to facilitate timely implementation. Electronic, results-based monitoring and evaluation systems were set up at the central and district levels. Supervision guidelines were developed for technical personnel as well as local school management committees in monitoring of community-led school reconstruction. Pictorial guidelines and video documentary were produced to show how to build remote schools with local materials safely.

Impact and results

Thousands of children were back into schools, vital government services and infrastructure restored to earthquake-affected communities, and jobs and income for families created by repairing critical road networks. ADB will continue its school reconstruction work under the Disaster Resilience of Schools Project approved in September 2018 that will support reconstruction of 174 schools, upgrade school infrastructure, and strengthen institutions for disaster risk management planning. The Earthquake Emergency Assistance Project was jointly financed by ADB, the United States Agency for International Development, and the Government of Nepal.

After the project, thousands of children were back in schools, and vital government services and infrastructure were restored.

ADB will continue its school reconstruction work under the Disaster Resilience of Schools Project where school infrastructure will be upgraded, and institutions for disaster risk management planning will be strengthened.

Lessons for replication

The school reconstruction project provided a significant, but unintended, added value for local communities. Many community members, particularly in rural areas, informally monitored contractors' work and observed the different earthquake resilience techniques used in construction. This raised awareness of construction quality among local people, and community members took key lessons for their own dwellings. This helped build more resilient communities.

> "
> *It's beautiful, strong, and has modern facilities... The teachers regularly use multimedia projectors in the classrooms, and it has made learning more fun and interesting.*
>
> **—Pratima Khadka, 14 years old, earthquake survivor, describing her newly reconstructed school**

Hashtags:

#Reconstruction, #Earthquake, #Education, #Nepal, #DisasterResponse #HumanCapital, #CapacityBuilding

Find out more:

- https://bit.ly/3aCfQeP

53

Small Hybrid Renewable Energy Systems Light Up Rural Communities

Project Name:	Improving Lives of Rural Communities Through Developing Small Hybrid Renewable Energy Systems
Country/Region:	Regional/Bangladesh, Maldives, Mongolia, Nepal, Pakistan, Sri Lanka, Tajikistan
Sector and Themes:	Energy
Year:	2009–2017
Project Leader:	Liping Zheng

The success of these pilots has led to similar projects being replicated in other rural areas and isolated islands in the region.

Development challenge

Almost 1 billion people in Asia and the Pacific still do not have continuous access to electricity. The varied terrain of countries in the region makes it technically and financially difficult to set up single interconnected power grids. Currently, most isolated rural areas rely on diesel power generation, which is frequently disrupted by fuel shortages, volatile oil prices, and inadequate maintenance of equipment. This creates a potential opportunity in these areas for renewable energy.

Solution

ADB's Private Sector Operations Department, South Asia Energy Division, East Asia Department, and the Regional and Sustainable Development Department worked together to pilot six small hybrid renewable energy projects. Of the six, three were implemented in remote island communities in Maldives and Sri Lanka, one in a remote mountain village in Nepal, one in a local school in Bangladesh, and one in a village in Pakistan.

Six pilot projects brought substantial tangible benefits to local communities, improved their livelihood, and resulted in lessons learned from implementation of these projects.

ADB provided technical expertise and financial support for the design, procurement, installation, and commissioning of the energy systems. ADB also trained and improved the capacity of the country's government officials, power sector engineers, and private sector to carry out efficient operations. ADB also provided institutional support in renewable energy policy development and capacity building in Mongolia and Tajikistan.

Knowledge products and services delivered

For each of the pilot projects, ADB provided a diagnostic study, which included a needs assessment, selection of locations, analysis of electricity demand patterns and load management requirements, assessment of renewable resources, technical and financial evaluation of the project, and environmental impact assessments. ADB helped conduct national and international workshops, conferences, and hands-on training programs on small renewable power systems.

Knowledge products included *Improving Lives of Rural Communities Through Developing Small Hybrid Renewable Energy Systems, Deployment of Renewable Energy Systems in Minigrids,* and *Excel-Based Toolkit for Planning Hybrid Energy Systems: User Guide,* which provided key insights and lessons learned covering aspects of planning, designing, procurement, installation, and operation and management of small hybrid renewable energy systems in rural areas and small isolated islands.

The project engaged rural communities, financial institutions, private sector partners, and nongovernment organizations for deployment of small hybrid renewable energy systems in rural areas.

Impact and results

With the additional supply of electricity, living conditions and quality of life greatly improved. The knowledge publications increased ADB's capacity and service offering in setting up solar photovoltaic and hybrid energy systems. The success of these pilots has led to similar projects being replicated in other Asian rural areas and isolated islands in the region. In Maldives, similar projects are being implemented under the Preparing the Outer Islands for Sustainable Energy Development Project. Energy projects in Bangladesh and Sri Lanka also have components that focus on setting up small hybrid wind turbines.

Lessons for replication

Lessons learned from the six pilot projects provide guidelines and best practices in setting up small wind, solar, and hybrid (wind, solar photovoltaic, and battery storage) renewable energy systems in varying terrains, and remote areas like islands and mountains.

The success of these pilots has led to similar projects being replicated in other Asian rural areas and isolated islands in the region.

Hashtags:
#RenewableEnergy, #WindEnergy, #SmallWindTurbines, #Maldives, #SriLanka, #Nepal, #Bangladesh, #Pakistan, #Mongolia, #Tajikistan

Find out more:
- https://bit.ly/2Xjv6KQ
- https://bit.ly/3vcGV1V
- https://bit.ly/3aBQZlc
- https://bit.ly/3BlOdwL

Policy Dialogue on Financial Restructuring of Tamil Nadu's Transmission Corporation

Project Name:	Chennai–Kanyakumari Industrial Corridor: Power Sector Investment Project.
Country/Region:	South Asia/India
Sector and Themes:	Energy
Year:	2018–Present
Project Leaders:	Pradeep Perera and Janardanam Srinivasan

The project highlights the importance and strength of the "One ADB" approach.

Development challenge

The Tamil Nadu Transmission Corporation (TANTRANSCO) faced critical risks to its financial sustainability as identified by ADB during the financial due diligence of the $451 million Chennai–Kanyakumari Industrial Corridor: Power Sector Investment Project.

Tamil Nadu's power sector was unbundled in 2010, and in 2015 the Tamil Nadu Electricity Board's assets and liabilities were allocated to successor companies, Tamil Nadu Generation and Distribution Company and TANTRANSCO. This saddled TANTRANSCO with liabilities that were unrelated to the transmission business and also made it ineligible for recovery through the transmission tariff. TANTRANSCO needed to maintain a certain debt–equity ratio under tariff regulations. As a result, TANTRANSCO had to borrow from commercial sources. Tamil Nadu's plans for investing in renewable energy depended on the fiscal sustainability of TANTRANSCO and its ability to invest in transmission infrastructure to provide connectivity to renewable energy.

Solution

ADB's South Asia Energy Division used its knowledge and experience of India's power sector, coupled with the financial management expertise of the ADB Procurement, Portfolio, and Financial Management Department, to identify the root causes of TANTRANSCO'S financial challenges and develop a pragmatic financial restructuring plan.

The project established an extra-high voltage transmission link to transfer extra capacity to Coimbatore, a major industrial center, and Chennai.

Knowledge products and services delivered

The project helped create a comprehensive financial restructuring plan and a financial management action plan to get TANTRANSCO back to fiscal sustainability in the medium term. These plans were approved by the Government of Tamil Nadu and they will strengthen TANTRANSCO's financial sustainability, financial management capacity, and corporate governance.

Gender-sensitive workplace practices were also introduced along with initiatives to enhance career opportunities for female staff. In addition, a framework was designed and implemented to improve TANTRANSCO's capacity to monitor the environmental and social impacts of transmission projects. ADB provided TA to help TANTRANSCO implement the financial restructuring plan to restore its financial sustainability and financial management action plan to improve corporate governance and financial management. Now, a series of measures are being introduced to improve the corporate governance and financial management capacity of TANTRANSCO.

Impact and results

Through the knowledge services provided under this project, ADB is helping the Government of Tamil Nadu effectively address legacy financial and debt issues, and improve the power sector's corporate governance and financial management capacity. The project has also incorporated gender-sensitive workplace practices. TANTRANSCO's capacity to monitor the environmental and social impacts of transmission projects was enhanced. The comprehensive financial restructuring plan designed by ADB, which includes an equity injection amounting to

A comprehensive financial restructuring plan and a financial management action plan developed through the project helped TANTRANSCO back to fiscal sustainability.

$3 billion from the state government, is expected to make TANTRANSCO financially viable by 2024. Encouraged by this initiative, the government of Tamil Nadu has requested that ADB help develop recommendations for financial restructuring and improved corporate governance of Tamil Nadu Generation and Distribution Company, which is also in dire financial straits.

Lessons for replication

The project highlights the importance and strength of the "One ADB" approach. Seamless and effective cooperation to integrate the power sector expertise of the South Asia Energy Division's knowledge and experience of India's power sector, coupled with the financial management expertise of the Procurement, Portfolio, and Financial Management Department, resulted in ADB obtaining the government buy-in for the financial restructuring plan for TANTRANSCO. This highlights the importance of internal knowledge collaboration that ADB can leverage, using its expertise, knowledge, and experience for successful project outcomes.

Hashtags:
#Energy, #India, #TamilNadu, #PolicyDialogue, #FinancialRestructuring, #InstitutionalStrengthening, #SouthAsia

Find out more:
- https://bit.ly/3jnBwjZ
- https://bit.ly/3aCiOQP
- https://bit.ly/2Xi1jII
- https://bit.ly/3mSpUq4

Winning the Fight Against Air Pollution in Ulaanbaatar

Project Name:	EARD Observations and Suggestions Policy Note Series: Winning the Fight Against Air Pollution in Ulaanbaatar
Country/Region:	East Asia/Mongolia
Sector and Themes:	Environment
Year:	2018-Present
Project Leader:	Pavit Ramachandran

The project will lead to the decarbonization of the energy system in the country with increased penetration of renewable energy.

Development challenge

Air pollution in Ulaanbaatar has escalated to alarming levels. Its impact goes beyond harmful and insidious health effects and has become a significant development challenge, resulting in enormous socioeconomic costs. These impacts are hardest felt by poor, the young, and the elderly.

Solution

Mongolia's challenge to reduce air pollution include data collection and monitoring, public awareness and government accountability, strengthened institutions, technology transfer, and financing mechanisms to support the transition to cleaner energy. ADB partnered with the Government of Mongolia in devising a $130 million policy development loan, approved in March 2018.

The loan set out to improve the efficiency of Mongolia's National Program for Reducing Air and Environmental Pollution 2017–2025 and the government's regulatory framework on air quality management. The support also helped to implement urgent measures to reduce air pollution and to protect human health. It established integrated energy and transport systems that were environmentally sound.

Knowledge products and services delivered

Complementing the loan program, ADB released a policy note Winning the Fight Against Air Pollution in Ulaanbaatar that offered long-term institutional recommendations to tackle air pollution. Best practices and experiences from other countries

Ulaanbaatar has suffered one of the highest levels of air pollution in the world, especially during wintertime when reliance on burning raw coal for heating homes was at its highest.

were studied for deriving lessons and specific policy actions that can work in Mongolia. It emphasized the importance of advocacy through public awareness and social pressure in ensuring government accountability. The note also furnished the government with a detailed list of short- and long-term policy recommendations.

Impact and results

In 2019, ADB approved a second, $160 million loan to support improved policies, regulatory and institutional capacity, and actions to tackle air pollution. In July 2020, ADB also approved loans totaling $43.65 million as part of a program to support the redevelopment of two additional subcenters in the eastern and western *ger* areas (a form of residential district consisting of parcels of land with one or more detached houses) of Ulaanbaatar. The financing is the third tranche of the Ulaanbaatar Urban Services and Ger Areas Development Investment Program, approved in 2013. ADB also extended a loan to the National Power Transmission Grid of Mongolia to install the country's first large-scale advanced battery energy storage system to accelerate the adoption of renewable energy. Evidence from winter 2019–2020 has shown a dramatic reduction in air pollution with particulate matter 2.5 falling by 42% from winter 2018–2019. The policy note continues to shape ADB's response and government policy.

Through ADB's help, the government is improving air quality management and has enacted measures to cut pollution and protect the health of the residents of the city.

Lessons for replication

ADB's use of policy-based lending proved to be successful. A dedicated knowledge product that brings together ADB's work in a clear and policy-relevant format had a major impact on the momentum of reform. The targeted approach to dissemination and including air pollution as the core policy challenge in the Mongolia chapter of the *Asian Development Outlook*, ensured that the messages were heard. The preparation of the note in the Mongolian language also greatly broadened the captured audience.

ADB's policy note offered long-term institutional recommendations to tackle air pollution, which continues to shape ADB's response and government policy.

> "
> *Air pollution poses severe health risks to people, especially children, in the Mongolian capital, while also burdening the country's already sluggish economic growth.*
>
> **—Maria Pia Ancora, senior urban development specialist, ADB**

Hashtags:

#AirPollution, #PolicyReforms, #Ger, #Mongolia, #AirQuality, #Health, #Urbanization

Find out more:

- https://bit.ly/3p2DtFQ

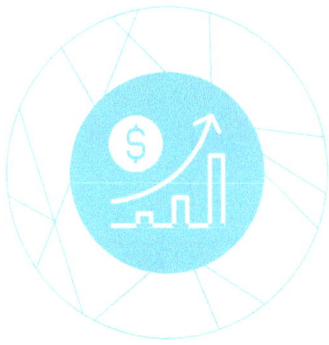

The Association of Southeast Asian Nations Infrastructure Centre of Excellence

Project Name: Regional Technical Assistance: Supporting Regional Project Development for Association of Southeast Asian Nations Connectivity

Region/Countries: Southeast Asia/Brunei Darussalam, Cambodia, Indonesia, Lao People's Democratic Republic, Malaysia, Philippines, Singapore, Thailand, and Viet Nam

Sector and Themes: Finance

Year: 2012–2019

Project Leader: Anouj Mehta

> *The launch of the two new facilities—Inclusive Finance Facility and ASEAN Catalytic Green Finance Facility—is timely and much needed.*
>
> **—Apisak Tantivorawong, minister of finance, Thailand**

ADB Principal Infrastructure Specialist Anouj Mehta and team in one of the seven high-level capacity building activities supported by the project. Singapore, July 2018.

Development challenge

Countries in the Association for Southeast Asian Nations (ASEAN) face two large and interlinked issues: massive infrastructure financing needs, and the need to better connect their population of more than 600 million. These countries required an estimated $60 billion per year between 2010 and 2020 and had a massive financing gap.[21] ADB was already involved in developing an ASEAN regional growth focus, and had contributed equity and management expertise to establish the ASEAN Infrastructure Fund in 2011. However, there was a huge challenge: attracting the scale of private capital.

Solution

The ASEAN Infrastructure Centre of Excellence (AICOE) was formulated as a facility available to all ASEAN countries. This regional TA was cofinanced by the governments of Singapore and Canada.

Knowledge products and services delivered

Twenty-three infrastructure projects in the energy, sanitation, health, and transport sectors across Cambodia, Indonesia, Malaysia, Philippines, Thailand, and Viet Nam were screened, leading to various sector-specific public–private partnership (PPP) models. Six PPP bid processes enhanced

---

[21]   ADB and ADB Institute. 2009. *Infrastructure for a Seamless Asia*. Manila.

the capacity of each of the governments. Seven high-level capacity building events, nine country workshops, and training sessions deepened the understanding of ASEAN government officials and stakeholders in designing and managing PPP and green and innovative finance project approaches. A "Beyond Traditional PPPs" model developed innovative forms of private capital mobilization, including green finance and capital market approaches. In all, six green and innovative financing concepts and structures were developed. A publication that included green and innovative finance models was disseminated at a 2019 ASEAN roundtable.

Impact and results

The Cambodia Solar Park project obtained the lowest bid of power tariff for a solar project in Southeast Asia. A second phase of the project is being supported by ADB. The project has both climate adaptation and mitigation impacts to help Cambodia meet its emission reduction commitments under the Paris Agreement. The ASEAN Scaling Up Renewable Energy Initiative program was initiated in 2019 to scale up the Cambodia project model across more countries, with three projects already commenced. Replicable PPP models were created for bus rapid transport, wastewater management, and health care, in three countries; capital market models led to bond issuances being supported by ADB's SERD Innovation Hub in Thailand and Indonesia.

The ASEAN Catalytic Green Finance (ACGF) Facility—the region's first regional green catalytic fund—was developed with AICOE support and launched in 2019 to accelerate green infrastructure

ADB Vice President Bambang Susantono promoted innovative finance mechanisms to accelerate green development at the Indonesia Green Finance Roundtable held in Jakarta, Indonesia in July 2018.

investments in Southeast Asia. The ACGF received almost $1.5 billion in cofinancing pledges from more than 10 partners. The first global ASEAN green finance conference held jointly by ADB and the Organisation for Economic Co-operation and Development in France in 2019 led to several follow-on programs in some ASEAN countries, which are currently supported by SERD.

Lessons for replication

The end-to-end support model used for the Cambodia solar park project and the PPP models for other sectors can be replicated for other infrastructure projects. Innovative financing models developed under the TA are also now being explored for other PPPs. The project also highlights the importance of building collaborative relationships with key government agencies, PPP units, and development partners. Partnerships with Canada and Singapore resulted in synergies with related initiatives such as the Asia-Pacific Project Preparation Facility.

"

We believe more governments in the region will adopt auction as a strategy to procure renewable energy generation capacity, and this structure and tariff will serve as a benchmark for future projects.

—Siddharta Shah, director, Office of Public–Private Partnerships, ADB

Hashtags:
#ASEAN, #Infrastructure, #PPP, #AICOE

Find out more:
- https://bit.ly/3FNNSuZ
- https://bit.ly/3mOhz6E
- https://bit.ly/3iYN4tF

ADB Promotes Gender Equality in Developing Member Countries

Project Name:	Trade Finance Program Gender Initiative
Country:	All Developing Member Countries
Sector and Themes:	Finance
Year:	2013–2020
Project Leaders:	Steven Beck, Can Sutken, Nana Khurodze, Keiko Nowacka, and Amanda Satterly

" *We need to recognize those who are making real changes to further equity in the workplace and encourage others to follow suit.*
—Can Sutken, Trade and Supply Chain Finance Program relationship manager, ADB "

Mutual Trust Bank Limited won the Gender Champion Award, which recognizes efforts to promote gender equity, at the 2018 TFP Awards in Singapore. The annual awards ceremony recognized 23 leading partner banks from 15 countries.

Development challenge

According to research by ADB, in Asia and the Pacific there is unmet demand for financial backing of $1.5 trillion in trade finance. Women-owned firms fare the worst, with 44% of requests for financial backing needs rejected. Women also continue to have an unequal share in senior management in the public and private sectors. Unless impediments to women's labor force participation and promotion opportunities are removed, the region will not realize its full potential. Closing the gender gap in leadership can lead to better business and financial outcomes.

Solution

The Trade and Supply Chain Finance Program (TSCFP) Gender Initiative, co-funded by ADB

and the Australian Department of Foreign Affairs and Trade, will result in more financial inclusion and support for individual women and women entrepreneurs. Nineteen of the trade finance partner banks in eight countries—Bangladesh, Kazakhstan, Mongolia, Myanmar, Pakistan, Samoa, Uzbekistan, and Viet Nam—participated in phase 1 (2017–2018) of the initiative by offering their human resource policies for analysis. In phase 2, a further 19 banks signed up and 5 banks are expected to implement the suggestions to attract, retain, and promote more women in banking. The TSCFP is also working to support banks in implementing the more challenging recommendations, like establishing grievance procedures and remedies around gender issues in the workplace, and equal pay. The third phase of the initiative will include activities for TSCFP partner banks: online training on gender-related topics, face-to-face training on eliminating gender bias, assistance to help banks develop gender-focused products, and assistance to selected banks with their efforts to achieve the Economic Dividends for Gender Equality certification.

Knowledge products and services delivered

The initiative supported the development of the ADB Private Sector and Gender Equity Thematic Group's first knowledge product, *Boosting Gender Equality Through ADB Trade Finance Partnerships*.[22] The aim of the initiative was to enable the participants to adopt and advance practical gender- and diversity-inclusive human resources policies and practices to increase the employment, retention, and progression of women within the workplace.

Impact and results

The project raised awareness of gender equality and surpassed its initial goal of having 8 banks implement at least one recommendation, with the implementation of 12 recommendations by 19 banks. TSCFP also collaborated with the ADB Sustainable Development and Climate Change Department on the TSCFP's Gender Champion Award.

Lessons for replication

To implement such a project in the future, support of women-led businesses should be the prime focus. Similar projects should anticipate a differing level of response, capability, and capacity among banks to implement recommendations to continue their gender equality journey.

In the photo (from left to right): Santosh Pokharel, ADB Relationship Manager; Saira Halai Chundrigar, General Manager - Relationship Management, Talent & Diversity, HBL; and Steven Beck, ADB Head of Trade and Supply Chain Finance. Photo taken on 3 September 2019 in Singapore at the 5th TFP Awards and Partners Dinner.

22   ADB. 2018. *Boosting Gender Equality Through ADB Trade Finance Partnerships*. Manila.

Women from Prime Bank Limited. The bank won the Best Green Deal Award (Issuing Bank) and Gender Champion Awards.

> *These measures have resulted in skill enhancements, boosting (women's) confidence to climb the career ladder and to continue excelling without giving in to societal barriers, stereotypes, and prejudices. Winning the Gender Champion Award will further inspire us to make new strides in gender equality and environmental sustainability.*
>
> **—Rahel Ahmed, managing director and chief executive officer, Prime Bank, Bangladesh**

Hashtags:

#WomenEmpowerment, #Feminism, #GenderEquality, #Pakistan, #Bangladesh, #Kazakhstan #Mongolia, #Samoa, #Uzbekistan, #VietNam

Find out more:

- https://bit.ly/30hSRDZ
- https://bit.ly/3mXwE5Q

Building an Ecosystem for Women Entrepreneurship in Sri Lanka

Project Name: Small and Medium-sized Enterprise Line of Credit Project

Region/Country: South Asia/Sri Lanka

Sector and Themes: Finance

Year: 2016–Present

Project Leader: Takuya Hoshino

> " *The We-Fi grant helps us to be more focused on lending to women entrepreneurs*
> —**Thusitha Nakandala, deputy general manager, Branch Banking, Sampath Bank, Sri Lanka** "

Women entreprenuers from Galle were among those 744 entrepreneurs from small and medium-sized enterprises across the county trained under the Small and Medium-Sized Enterprises Line of Credit Project.

Development challenge

Despite their significant role, small and medium-sized enterprises (SMEs) in Sri Lanka are constrained by limited access to bank finance. Women, who tend to run smaller businesses without collateral, are disproportionately impacted. Banks need an incentive to reach out to female SME owners and women need a more enabling environment to signal their competency and ability to repay loans.

Solution

In 2016, through 10 participating banks with 80% market share, ADB introduced a line of credit targeting lending to women-led SMEs. This credit line was complemented with TA from the Japan Fund for Poverty Reduction for training and networking opportunities to women entrepreneurs in the export-oriented sectors. This TA also designed an SME credit guarantee institution, which provides a solution for women-led SMEs lacking collateral by promoting cash flow-based lending by banks. In 2018, the original project received an additional boost with a $12.6 million grant from the Group of 2020 Women Entrepreneurs Finance Initiative (We-Fi), which enhanced the project's gender dimensions.

Knowledge products and services delivered

The project delivered business development training for women entrepreneurs, seminars on raising awareness of women entrepreneurship, and access to start-up finance. It fosters increased knowledge through an online platform for learning and mentoring. The project also organized ICT and business process management-related career events specifically for women. In addition to carrying out a policy study on establishing an SME credit guarantee institution, the project conducted gender gap assessments for three government organizations to develop a new institutional framework for the capacity development of women.

Impact and results

As of December 2020, a credit line of $175 million had been disbursed to 3,546 SMEs, out of which 1,338 were women-led. Because of the project's success, the government requested a $165 million additional loan, which was approved by ADB in November 2020. The project will continue to 2023. A total of $24.4 million in loans, cofinanced with $6.5 million from the We-Fi grant, was provided to 663 women-led SMEs. Out of 663 We-Fi beneficiaries, 231 were first-time borrowers and 139 were in economically lagging regions (Northern, Eastern, Sabaragamuwa, and Uva regions), and 39 trained women accessed We-Fi grants.

About 750 female entrepreneurs received training, which shifted to an online format in 2020 due to COVID-19. Most of the business plans the participants designed were rated viable by banks. Career events at Matugama and Galle in 2018

Nelum Devi, owner of Nelum Plant Nursery.

Women designing saree from Indu Mala Saloon.

> *I started this business with a small investment, SLRs,000 ($50). I have taken this to greater heights over the years. I have also created employment. This makes me proud. Any woman can start a venture of her own even in a small way and realize their goals.*
> **—Indumala Rajapaksha, Sarees and Salon, Kandy and Colombo**

targeted at employing female students in the ICT sector attracted 1,641 students. Three government organizations and two civil society organizations are developing policies to mainstream gender-responsive banking practices. The success of the project with We-Fi grant support has resulted in similar programs being designed for Fiji, Papua New Guinea, and Viet Nam.

Lessons for replication

Engaging a wide range of stakeholders such as banks, government organizations, and chambers of commerce, is important. These relationships take years to build. Data collection at the micro level is critical to understand the lending practices of participating financial institutions and to provide credible policy advice. Government ownership is critical for the successful implementation, creation of knowledge, and application into practices for sustainable transformation. High-level strategic guidance within the government should be in place to identify key issues to be resolved with ADB's

knowledge support. A government officer should be appointed to provide constructive inputs in ADB's knowledge products throughout the implementation.

Ruchirani Munasinghe, owner of Negambo Farm.

> "
> *The agricultural instructor advised me to attend a training program by ADB. ADB's training program invited bank officials. I learned a lot about management there. After the training I went to several banks with my business proposal to borrow. I wasn't afraid.*
> **—Ruchirani Munasinghe, owner of Negambo Farm, Anuradhapura**

Hashtags:
#SriLanka, #SME, #SMECredit, #SouthAsia, #Gender, #WomenEntrepreneur, #CapacityBuilding

Find out more:
• https://bit.ly/3mVDSr5

Promoting Green and Innovative Finance Across Southeast Asia

Project Name:	The Innovation Hub and The ASEAN Catalytic Green Finance Facility
Country:	Southeast Asia
Sector and Themes:	Finance
Year:	2018–Present
Project Leader:	Anouj Mehta

> *For the global COVID-19 recovery to safeguard against future pandemics, drive sustainable growth, jobs, and investment, it has to be green. Green finance, green systems, green policies. Now is the chance to do better for people and the planet.*
> —**Jorge Moreira da Silva, director, Development Co-operation Directorate, Organisation for Economic Co-operation and Development**

The SERD Innovation Hub, was set up in 2018 to develop green and bankable innovative finance projects that can catalyze private, commercial, and institutional capital for each dollar of sovereign finance.

Development challenge

The Southeast Asia region has rapidly depleting natural resources due to pollution and unsustainable use, and huge climate change vulnerabilities. Estimates indicate a 60% higher regional carbon footprint by 2050, and regional climate change impacts are expected to cause an almost 11% drop in gross domestic product (GDP) by 2100 from impacts on agriculture, health, ecosystems, and labor productivity. The region requires an estimated $210 billion annually from 2016 to 2030 in investments for climate-resilient infrastructure. However, there is an estimated $102 billion per year financing deficit.

Solution

The SERD Innovation Hub, one of the first in ADB with an innovative finance focus, was set up in 2018 to develop green and bankable innovative finance projects that can catalyze private, commercial, and institutional capital for each dollar of sovereign finance. The Innovation Hub's activities are underpinned by a regional project, the Green and Innovative Finance Initiative for Scaling Up Southeast Asian Infrastructure (GIF), and a vision and strategic road map for its activities.

Knowledge products and services delivered

In its 2 years of operations, the SERD Innovation Hub has delivered across five planned activity pillars:

i.   creation of a pool of experts and TA fund;

ii.   copious knowledge- and capacity-building events, training, and publications;

iii. development of innovative finance concepts and pilot projects;

iv.   establishment of global partnerships for knowledge and cofinancing commitments; and

v.   the first regional green fund of $1.5 billion, the ASEAN Catalytic Green Finance (ACGF) Facility. This fund was developed and launched in 2019, to support ASEAN member states to source public and private financing for infrastructure projects that promote environmental sustainability and contribute to climate change goals. In its first year of operations the ACGF

approved 4 green projects worth $1.4 billion. The project formalized 13 partnerships for knowledge, capacity, and project development. It also mobilized emergency supplies to respond to the COVID-19 pandemic in just 3 days, implementing distribution over 2 months for more than 800,000 people in the Philippines in an innovative collaboration with government, private sector, and national government entities.

Impact and results

The SERD Innovation Hub has helped change the mindset for green and innovative finance across ADB, with the ACGF a highly visible and pioneering focus for the bank. A major success in the era of COVID-19 has been green bond market development, with support for the successful issuance of the Thailand Sustainability and Social bonds in late 2020. The Innovation Hub is also now supporting bonds development in Indonesia and the Philippines. ADB approval of green and innovative projects achieved with the hub's support are a model for effective leveraging of funding to meet climate objectives.

Lessons for replication

The operation of the hub has shown how collaboration is critical to meet emerging challenges faced by the region. Regional departments must be proactive in identifying new and emerging opportunities to support, one key example being the promotion of green recovery strategies. An internal pool of experts within the SERD Innovation Hub team has proved crucial in applying specific key performance indicators such as green criteria at a project level, as this a fundamental element for green projects and requires extra effort and analysis.

ASEAN CATALYTIC GREEN FINANCE FACILITY 2019–2020
Accelerating Green Finance in Southeast Asia
JANUARY 2021

ACGF ADB

Former ADB President Takehiko Nakao (standing, fifth from left), Thailand Minister of Finance Apisak Tantivorawong (standing, sixth from left), ASEAN Ministers of Finance and senior officials, and representatives from development and private sector partners during the launch of the ASEAN Catalytic Green Finance Facility in Chiang Rai, Thailand.

Now is the right time to strengthen the ASEAN Catalytic Green Finance Facility's role within the fund. Going forward, vehicles like this will be key to continue supporting a green recovery from COVID-19.

—Brahmantio Isdijoso, chair, ASEAN Infrastructure Fund and director of Government Support and Infrastructure Financing Management, Ministry of Finance, Indonesia

Hashtags:
#GreenInfrastructure, #Sustainability, #Infrastructure, #PrivateCapital, #ClimateChange #CapacityBuilding, #Innovation, #ACGF

Find out more:
- https://bit.ly/2Xdxltw
- https://bit.ly/3lHnuLq
- https://bit.ly/2YUHD8c
- https://bit.ly/3AIGE7O
- https://bit.ly/2Xdxltw
- https://bit.ly/30jgtrQ
- https://bit.ly/2YNa1lX

Turning off the Tap for Money Laundering and Terrorism

Project Name: Anti-Money Laundering/Countering the Financing of Terrorism

Region/Country: Regional/All Developing Member Countries

Sector and Themes: Finance

Year: 2018–Present

Project Leader: Steven Beck

The trade and finance scorecard is the start of a process of engagement on this difficult subject.

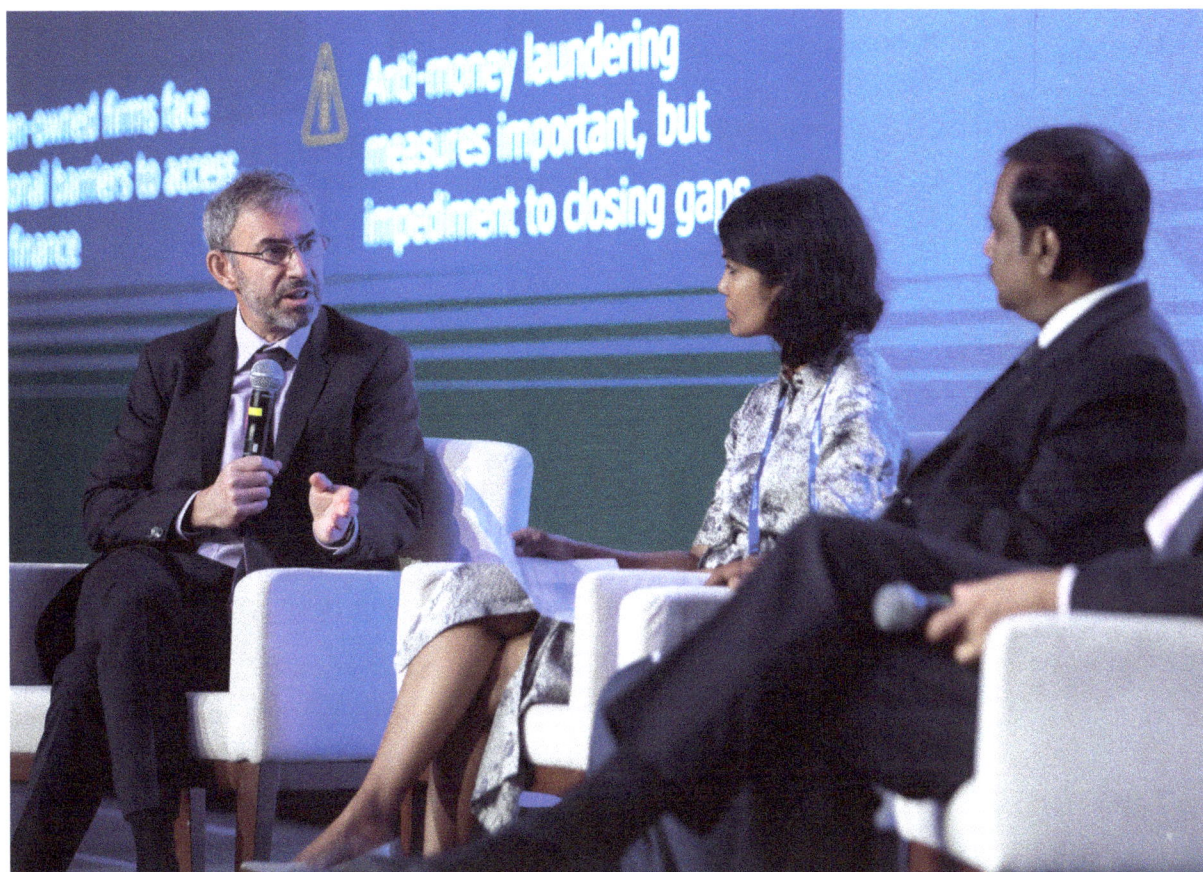

The Singapore launch of the 2019 ADB Trade Finance Gaps, Growth, and Jobs Survey held at the annual Global Trade Review Asia-Pacific Conference. ADB TSCFP Head Steven Beck moderated a panel that discussed how anti-money-laundering measures can be an impediment to closing gaps in financing and presented policy recommendations that would effectively fight financial crimes while promoting financial inclusion.

Development challenge

Efforts to stop financial crime can unintentionally lead to legitimate SMEs, including those in emerging markets, being unable to find the support they need to grow, create jobs, and contribute to development. The Trade Finance Gaps, Growth, and Jobs Survey published in 2019 by ADB's TSCFP identified unintended consequences of anti-money laundering regulatory compliance as a major impediment to closing the $1.5 trillion trade finance gap particularly among SMEs.

Solution

ADB's TSCFP developed knowledge initiatives to address the problem: a market-based solution that improves reporting requirements that could help thwart crime; online training and certification for professionals in anti-money laundering and counter-financing of terrorism (AML/CFT); a Trade Finance Scorecard; and a webinar series in the Pacific on best practices. With banks, regulators, and international organizations, TSCFP created a plan to improve detection, investigation, and prosecution of trade-based money laundering and to reduce unintended adverse consequences on access to trade financing due to compliance requirements. This led to the creation of data elements for suspicious activities reports provided by banks to regulators and use of a feedback loop to determine which elements from those reports are useful. TSCFP, in partnership with goAML—a fully integrated reporting system developed by the United Nations Office on Drugs and Crime used in about 50 jurisdictions—is implementing these data elements.

TSCFP is providing online training and certification to banks in partnership with the Association of Certified Anti-Money Laundering Specialists. About 700 bankers in developing member countries have taken part in three levels of AML courses. In December 2020 TSCFP hosted a Pacific AML/CFT Webinar series with about 2,000 participants in its 5-day discussion and knowledge sharing on existing and emerging financial crime issues in the Pacific. The Trade Finance Scorecard identifies seven systemic elements of effective regulation that could be strengthened to mitigate the risk and unintended consequences of AML/CFT regulations. The scorecard assesses five transaction issues stemming from the interpretation, implementation, and compliance of AML/CFT regulations.

Knowledge products and services delivered

TSCFP identified trade-relevant data points to be added to existing suspicious activities report templates. The feedback mechanism between regulators and banks helped determine if data elements from suspicious activity reports can be used effectively to handle financial crimes. TSCFP also trained and certified bank professionals in AML/CFT issues and developed the Trade Finance Scorecard.

Impact and results

ADB's initiatives around trade-based money laundering data points and feedback mechanisms were cited as best practice in the December 2020 Financial Action Task Force-Egmont Group trade-based money laundering report.[23] ADB gathered support from the financial intelligence units in seven countries—Bangladesh, Indonesia, Mongolia, Nepal,

Former U.S. Department of Treasury Undersecretary Sigal Mandelker was the keynote speaker at the March 2019 AML-CFT in Trade Workshop organized by the ADB Trade and Supply Chain Finance Program. The event was a follow-up to the Trade Finance Scorecard: Regulation and Market Feedback publication and was attended by stakeholders from the private and public sectors as well as and international organizations.

---

[23] FATF - Egmont Group. 2019. *Trade-Based Money Laundering: Trend and Development.* Paris.

New Zealand, Pakistan, and Sri Lanka—to bring the discussion to the International Users Group of the United Nations Office on Drugs and Crime's goAML system.

Lessons for replication

The project demonstrates the need to attack problems from different fronts and involve market participants, regulators, and ADB to enact change. It shows that knowledge products and market testing can become a feedback loop for improvements.

> *Preventing criminals and terrorists from exploiting the global financial system is critically important... But these regulations can also undermine jobs and growth at small businesses and [in] developing countries. This new scorecard will open a channel of dialogue among stakeholders to help prevent crime and terrorism while financing growth and job creation.*
>
> **—Steven Beck, head of trade and supply chain finance, ADB**

Hashtags:
#Regional, #TradeFinance, #AntiMoneyLaundering, #CounteringTerrorism, #Scorecard

Find out more:
- https://bit.ly/3ALrnDn
- https://bit.ly/2YXWJtF
- https://bit.ly/3ALrnDn
- https://bit.ly/3DLqqwy

Quantifying Global Market Gaps for Trade Finance

Project Name:	2019 Trade Finance Gaps, Growth, and Jobs Survey
Region/Country:	Global
Sector and Themes:	Finance
Year:	2019
Project Leaders:	Steven Beck and Kijin Kim

ADB's trade finance survey is a unique tool helping quantify trade finance market trends and gaps in provision, by region, as well as reasons behind them.
—Marc Auboin, counselor for trade finance and coherence, World Trade Organization

ADB Trade and Supply Chain Finance Head Steven Beck presented the results of the 2019 Trade Finance Gap, Growth, and Jobs Survey at the GTR Asia 2019 in Singapore.

Development challenge

Since 80%–90% of global trade relies on trade finance, any gap in availability of financing is a threat to achieving the SDGs. A trade financing gap has a direct effect on global economic growth and particularly impacts SMEs.

Solution

In 2019, ADB's ADB's Private Sector Operations Department, through its Trade and Supply Chain Finance Program, and the Economic Research and Regional Cooperation Department (ERCD) spearheaded a survey to help gauge the size of the trade finance shortfall and its expected impact. Before this study, there was no quantifiable information on market gaps for trade finance. This knowledge product is particularly useful for policy makers and the private sector to understand why the gap exists and identify actions to close it. The *2019 Trade Finance Gaps, Growth, and Jobs Survey*[24] found that there was a $1.5 trillion market gap in trade financing. The study found that SME applications have a 45% rejection rate versus 39% for medium-sized and larger firms, and 17% for multinational corporations. Women entrepreneurs face a 44% rejection rate, compared with 38% for male-owned firms. The study also explored the leading causes for the gap, which were AML and know-your-customer regulations. While such regulations are crucial to ensure the global financial system is not used to fund terrorism or launder money, they can

---

[24] ADB. 2019. ADB Briefs: 2019 Trade Finance Gaps, Growth, and Jobs Survey. Manila.

inadvertently sever legitimate companies in less developed markets from the financial support they need to grow.

Knowledge products and services delivered

A brief report explained how trade finance is essential in meeting the SDGs. It highlighted the unrealized potential of digital technology to narrow gaps particularly among SMEs, and how women-owned firms access trade finance. It looked at the role of financial technology and digitization in boosting growth and efficiency for women-owned firms.

The TSCFP and ERCD launched efforts directed at closing the gap, including the Anti-Money Laundering and Counter-Terrorism Financing Initiative. They organized seminars and workshops,

and wrote blog posts to build capacity in the banking sector and thus reduce the trade gap. It promoted a digitization initiative to use technology that would increase access to trade finance in DMCs. The survey results were also disseminated at the Asia-Pacific Trade Facilitation Forum 2019.[25]

Impact and results

The gap study is the first of its kind and has been widely cited by other institutions and publications. It quantifies market gaps and brings them to the attention of regulatory, academic, and policy making bodies, adding a sense of urgency and a call to action. As the trade gap mostly affects emerging markets, TSCFP's partner banks, SMEs, and, more broadly, ADB's developing member countries benefit from efforts to address the reasons for these gaps.

The launch of the 2019 Trade Finance Gaps, Growth, and Jobs Survey was held at the GTR Asia 2019 in Singapore attended by over 1,000 participants. In the panel with ADB Steven Beck were Marc Auboin, Counsellor, World Trade Organization; Mohanavelu Muthukrishnan, BNY Mellon; and Kaushalya Somasundaram, fintech expert.

---

[25] ESCAP. 2019. *Asia-Pacific Trade Facilitation Forum 2019*. 17-18 September. Bangkok.

Lessons for replication

This survey led by ADB resulted from collaboration with several private and public partner organizations, which helped circulate the questionnaire through their member banks and firms. Such collaborative efforts are critical in getting quality responses from as many respondents as possible.

The study estimates a $1.5 trillion market gap, impeding ability to achieve the SDGs. The study recommended specific actions to address the gap. ADB's TFP does about 4,000 deals valued at over $6 billion every year to close gaps and is the largest mobilizer of cofinance at ADB.

> *The survey enables us to put dimensions around the challenges and those dimensions allow agencies like ours to promote an appropriate response from the development community. This extends up to the level of the United Nations Secretary General, who has now included access to affordable trade financing as a major SDG priority.*
>
> **—Ian Sayers, senior advisor, Access to Financing, International Trade Centre, Geneva**

Hashtags:
#TradeFinance, #Trade, #Finance, #Tradeflows, #PovertyReduction, #FinTech, #Women

Catalyzing Climate Finance for Better Infrastructure and Business in Shandong, People's Republic of China

Project Name:	Catalyzing Climate Finance: Shandong Green Development Fund Project
Region/Country:	East Asia/People's Republic of China
Sector and Themes:	Finance
Year:	2019–Present
Project Leader:	Leung Kang Hang

This is the first project by ADB in the field of green finance to establish a green fund with loans from international financial organizations.

Shandong province in the People's Republic of China has the country's highest greenhouse gases emissions and faces multiple climate vulnerability challenges.

Development challenge

Shandong is one of the focus provinces in the People's Republic of China (PRC) that was selected to pilot the government's paradigm shift under the 13th Five-Year Plan—from a GDP development orientation to a development model centered on quality growth. Shandong has the country's highest greenhouse gases emissions and faces multiple climate vulnerability challenges. The province is required to reduce its carbon dioxide emission intensity by 20.5% by 2020. Shandong also aims to achieve peaking of carbon dioxide emissions around 2027, or 3 years earlier than the national goal. The province faces many challenges in meeting these goals due to heavy reliance on coal and increasing traffic: in 2017, the provincial capital Jinan was ranked as the most congested city in the PRC.

Traditional sovereign financing and banking systems have little incentive to cater to climate change investment. A new approach is needed to unlock significant climate finance for cities, especially from private, institutional, and commercial sources.

Solution

The Shandong Green Development Fund (SGDF) Project was initiated to catalyze capital for the development of climate-positive infrastructure and business.

The project comprises a mix of $1.2 billion in public and private sector capital, and $300 million in catalytic resources from international financing institutions. Executed by the Shandong Provincial Government and implemented by the Shandong Development and Investment Holding Group, the project will finance a portion of the total capital expenditures of selected climate-positive subprojects for a capped period to make the subprojects bankable, by addressing the upfront project risks, as well as promoting advanced technologies and an integrated approach for climate change. The subprojects will be screened and selected with climate criteria and performance established in the SGDF Green Climate Assessment Guidelines, which is in line with the Green Climate Fund investment framework. It is the first climate fund in the PRC to be categorized as having effective gender mainstreaming.

Knowledge products and services delivered

The project produced its first publication, an ADB brief titled *Catalyzing Climate Finance with the Shandong Green Development Fund*,[26] which describes the national climate policy context, explains the selection of Shandong to pilot the study and its climate finance priorities, and describes ADB's role, the project development objectives, structure, investment strategy, project selection criteria, and its initial project pipeline.

Impact and results

The SGDF will be structured as an investment pooling vehicle for climate financing. By 2030, the project is expected to reduce carbon dioxide-equivalent emissions by 3.75 million tons per year and directly build resilience for 7.5 million people in Shandong

The project will help reduce carbon dioxide-equivalent emissions and directly build resilience for 7.5 million people in Shandong province by 2040.

[26] ADB. 2020. *Catalyzing Climate Finance with he Shandong Green Development Fund. ADB Briefs.* No. 144. Manila

province by 2040. The executing and implementing agencies have mobilized staff and fund management company CICC Capital Management Co. Ltd. to undertake start-up activities including operations setup, discussions with private sector investors, subproject sourcing, agreements preparation, and obtain related clearances as needed. The project helped in preparing the SGDF Green Climate Assessment Guidelines, the cost estimates, and the climate mitigation and adaptation benefits on 10 project concepts, including three pre-feasibility studies.

Lessons for replication

The study identified key areas for policy action including creating an enabling environment to cater to climate financing requirements for longer term, and building up climate finance capacity and knowledge. These policies will help overcome barriers in climate finance.

The project will help promote advanced technologies and an integrated approach for climate change.

Hashtags:
#ClimateChange, #ClimateFinance, #SDG, #Strategy2030, #Shandong #Collaboration, #Investment

Mapping the COVID-19 Supply Chain

Project Name:	Capacity Development for the Supply Chain Finance Program
Region/Country:	Regional/All Developing Member Countries
Sector and Themes:	Finance
Year:	2020
Project Leader:	Steven Beck

Countries can use the tool to effectively plan for their supply of medical products to tackle the COVID-19 pandemic.

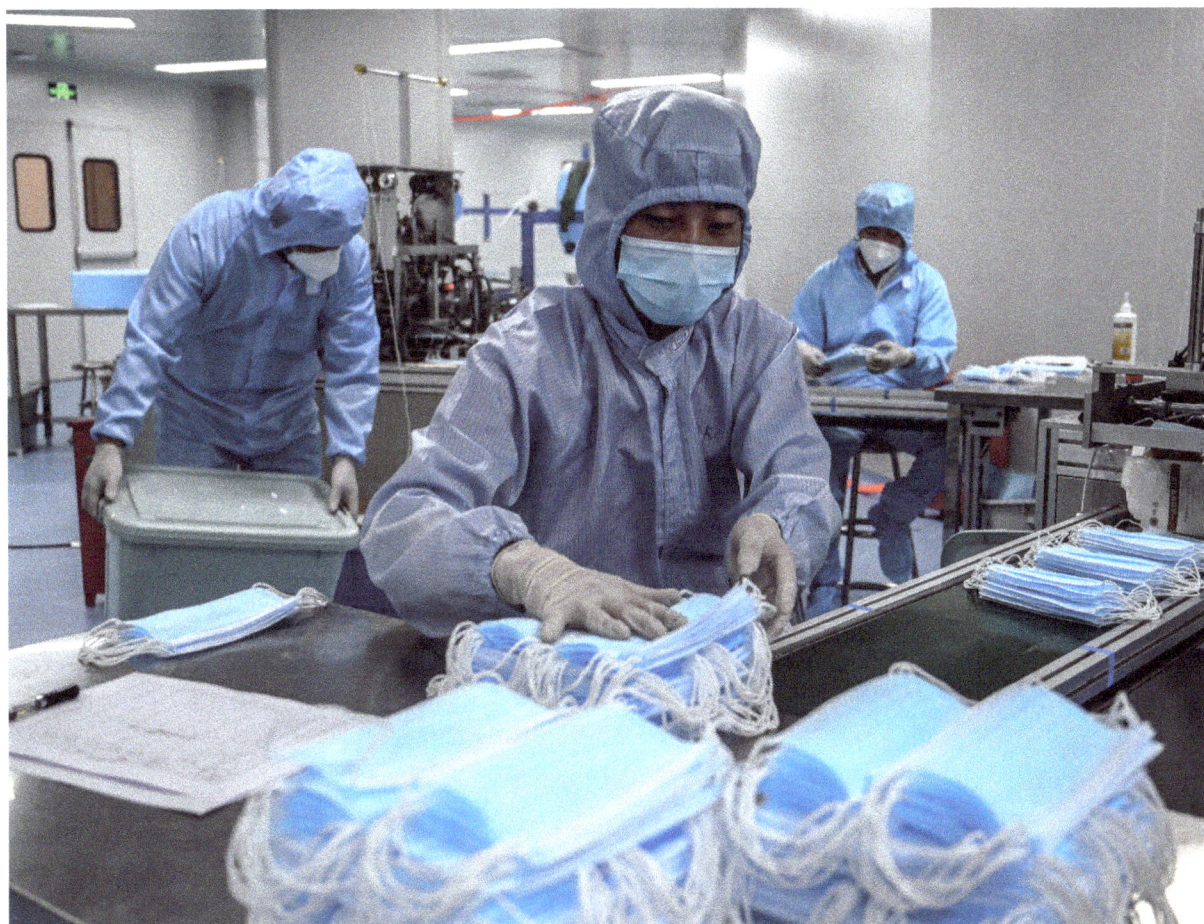

The COVID-19 pandemic forced manufacturing facilities and global supply chains to shut down or operate at reduced capacities.

Development challenge

With globalization, businesses and their supply chains have become extremely interconnected and complex. The COVID-19 pandemic forced manufacturing facilities and global supply chains to shut down or operate at reduced capacities. In the health sector, the pandemic spurred demand for critical medical equipment like ventilators, personal protective equipment, and medicines. However, governments, investors, and others concerned were unable to easily find information on companies in the health supply chain, the products they manufacture, and supply chains they use. ADB's TSCFP identified this information gap and saw the need to fix it so that slowdowns or blockages in the supply chains of key medical products could be addressed and the recovery from COVID-19 could be sped up.

Solution

ADB's TSCFP team created an interactive mapping tool that allows governments, banks, investors, health care professionals, and companies to trace the supply chains of critical medical products such as masks, ventilators, and personal protective equipment. This initiative came into being alongside the $20 billion committed by ADB to fight COVID-19 and offset its global economic impact. The database has information on more than 25,000 companies involved in health supply chains.

Knowledge products and services delivered

The TA supported an interactive mapping tool to trace supply chains of medical products and put on tap critical information that has benefited many health care companies. In particular, the tool allows countries to trace the supply chains of 34 critical medical products, including goods related to vaccines. Countries can determine the name, location, turnover, and other details of the companies involved in each part of the supply chain. They can then use this information to inform their medical resource sourcing strategy, and effectively plan for their supply of medical products to tackle the COVID-19 pandemic.

Impact and results

Banks, governments, other international organizations, and companies have used the tool to search out opportunities or to offset problems within global health supply chains. The tool now includes visual representation of vaccine trade flows from one country to another, and also features the latest news to help identify blockages that impede the supply chain of vaccine and cold chain distribution. The TSCFP is also considering additional uses for the tool in investigating the supply chains for non-COVID-related products.

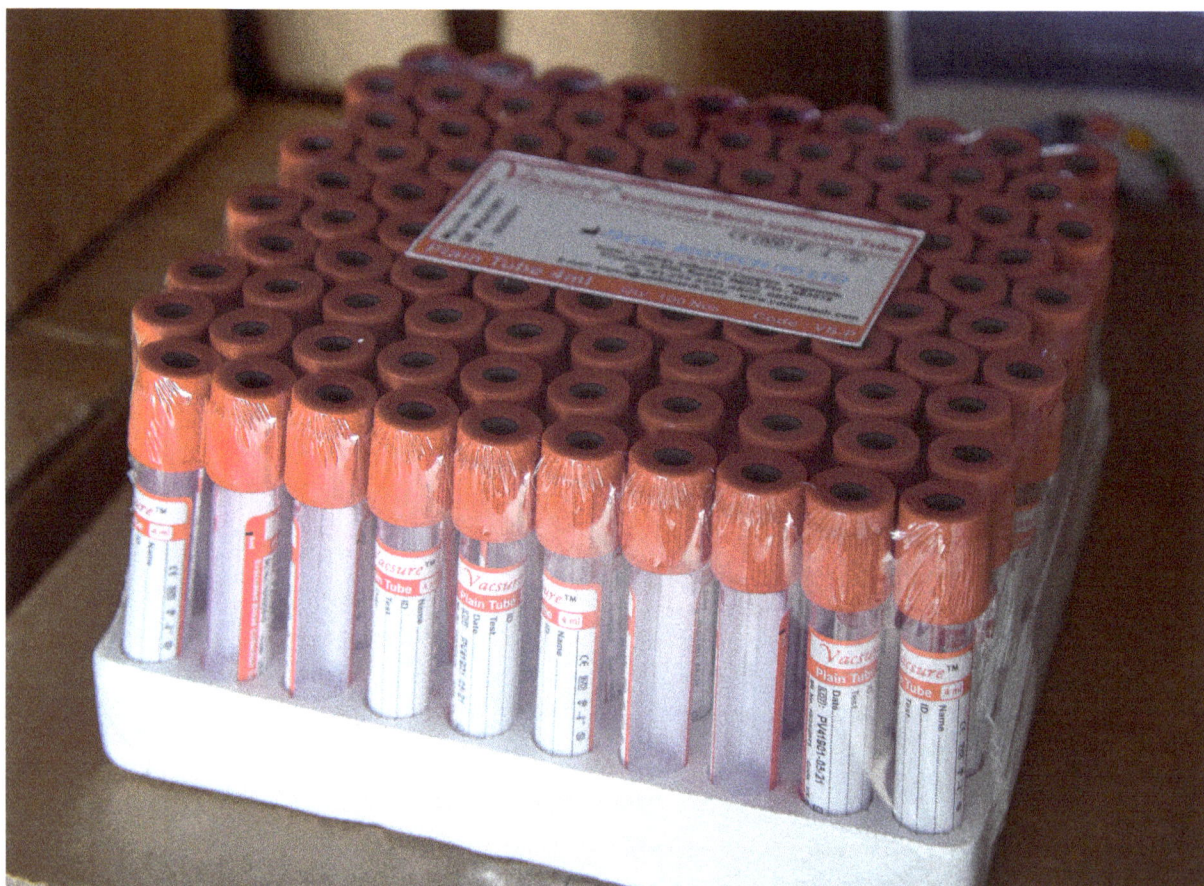

Through the TA, an interactive mapping tool was developed to help trace supply chains of medical products.

Lessons for replication

The experience with the mapping tool demonstrates the importance of knowledge products to achieve effective development results. The mapping tool shows that ADB's experience—in this case its relationships with banks and other players in global supply chains—can be leveraged to both discover and address issues with widespread negative implications.

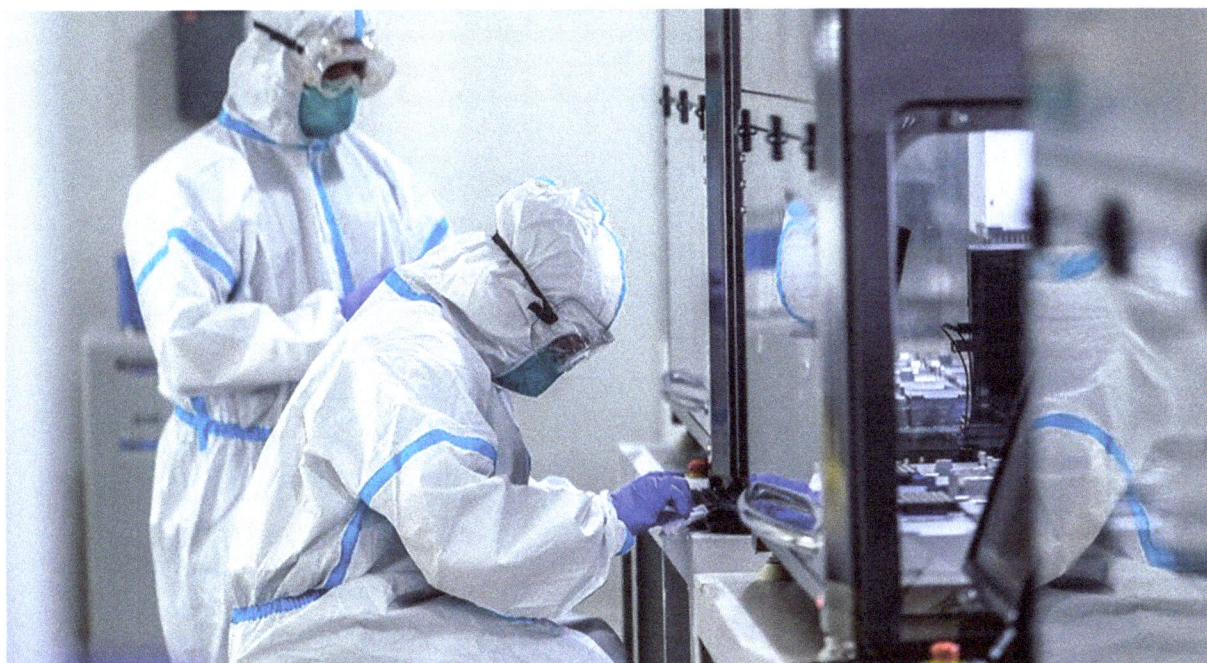

Information from the interactive mapping tool helped to effectively plan for the supply of medical products to tackle the COVID-19 pandemic.

Hashtags:

#ClimateChange, #ClimateFinance, #SDG, #Strategy2030, #Shandong #Collaboration, #Investment

Find out more:

- https://www.adb.org/multimedia/scf

Better Woman and Child Health Development in Uzbekistan

Project Name: Woman and Child Health Development Project

Region/Country: Central and West Asia/Uzbekistan

Sector and Themes: Health

Year: 2004–2012

Project Leader: Nargiza Parkhatovna Talipova

> " *The project was the first to develop a series of evidence-based clinical guidelines for the management and prevention of complications that cause maternal mortality.* "
> **—Klara Yadgarova, head, Main Department of Maternal and Child Healthcare, Ministry of Health in 2004–2009**

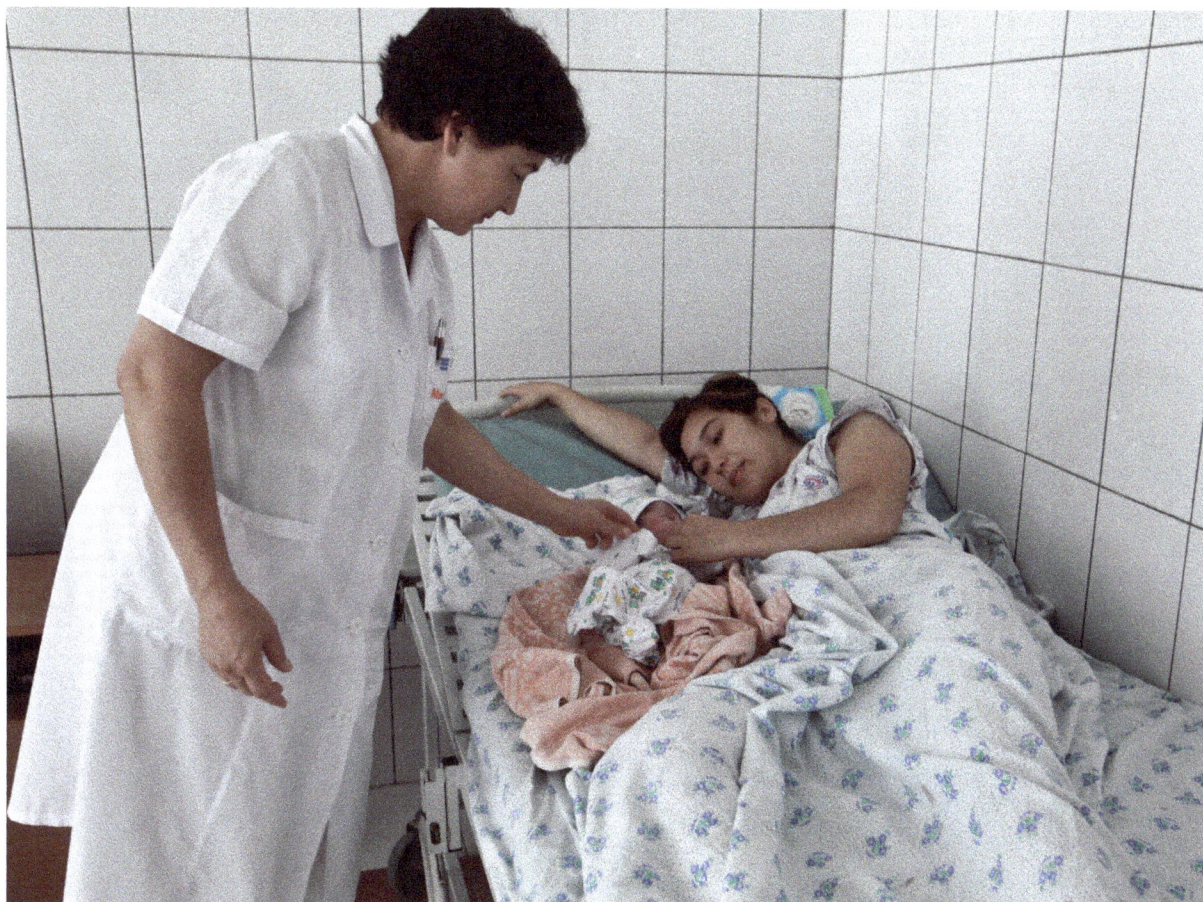

Infectious disease is one of the causes of health vulnerabilities among pregnant women and newborns in Uzbekistan.

Development challenge

In Uzbekistan, infectious diseases, poor use of contraceptives among women, and reduced iron deficiency anemia among pregnant women resulted in health vulnerabilities for women and newborns.

Solution

Together with the government, ADB and the World Bank jointly developed complementary projects to support primary health care and health financing in Uzbekistan. These efforts complemented ongoing health projects and tapped the expertise and activities of the United Nations and bilateral agencies already involved in maternal, newborn, and child health.

ADB's support focused on strengthening decentralized woman and child health services; strengthening finance, information, and management; building a blood safety program; and improving project management. The Woman and Child Development project[27] aimed to strengthen the primary health care system and first referral network for women and child health. The government worked on reconstructing maternal care facilities, the World Bank supported building and upgrading primary care centers, and ADB focused on equipping women and child health facilities. The project also introduced a national blood safety program and supported restructuring of the blood transfusion supply system. The project also

27 ADB. 2004. *Report and Recommendation of the President to the Board Directors: Proposed Loan and Technical Assistance Grant to the Republic of Uzbekistan for the Women and Child Health Development Project.* Manila.

supported the development of a local network in the Ministry of Health with establishment of a data processing and ICT center.

Knowledge products and services delivered

The project recognized that training health care professionals at all levels was critical to the project's success. The project provided clinical guidelines for health care practitioners and developed a nursing degree program. It upgraded the curriculum for nurses and doctors to international standards; trained more than 3,500 women and child health specialists at training centers; and delivered courses for 20,000 primary health care nurses. It trained 1,870 national, provincial, and district specialists in blood safety in collaboration with the World Health Organization (WHO) and the United States Centers for Disease Control and Prevention.

Results

Since 2004, Uzbekistan's mortality rates have fallen by more than 37%, while for infants the rate has fallen by more than 33%, mostly due to improved perinatal and neonatal care services. The project also established six regional blood transfusion centers with modern equipment and facilities. Today all blood samples are screened for infectious diseases before transfusion, compared to only 60% in 2000.

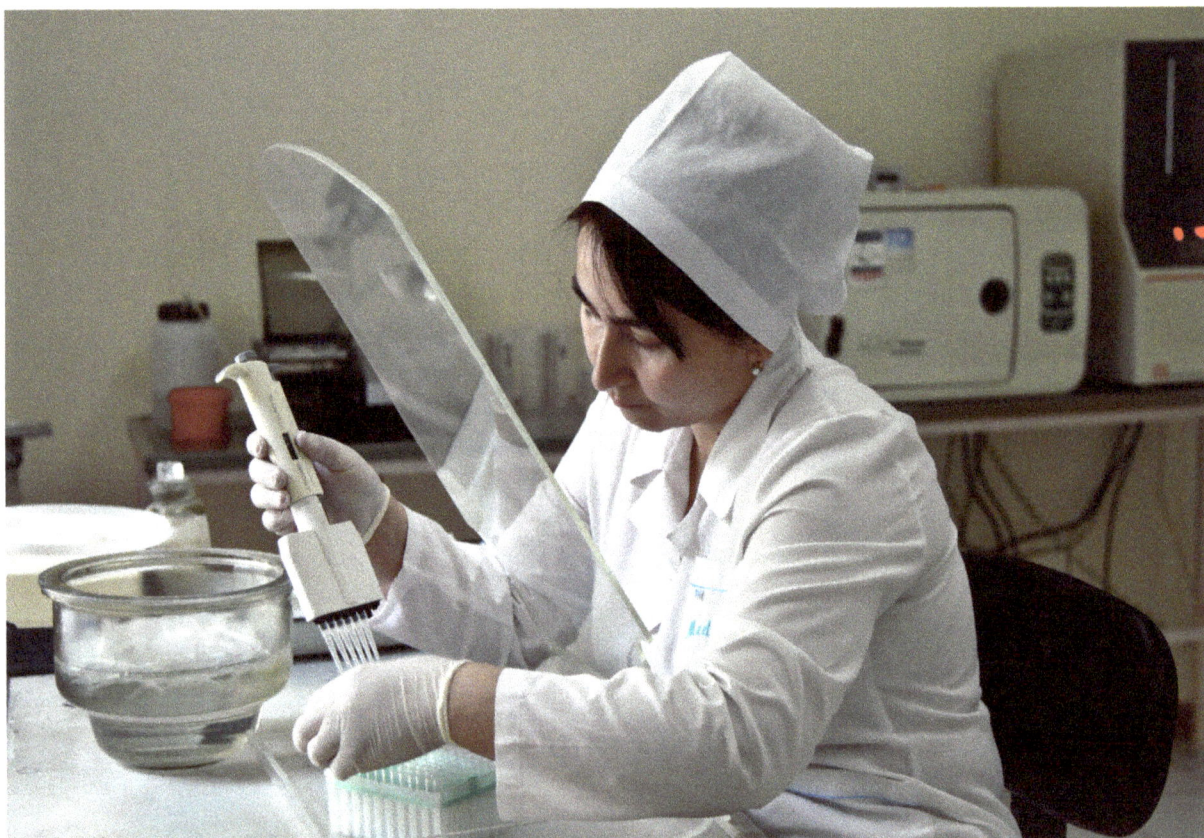

Training health care professionals at all levels is critical.

Lessons for replication

The project provides important lessons about strong commitment by government as well as close donor collaboration in complementing each other's efforts in ongoing health projects and tapping upon peer sector expertise. The project also emphasized the criticality of training health care professionals at all levels in the use of new equipment and the latest methods in maternal and child health care for effective implementation and delivery of similar health projects.

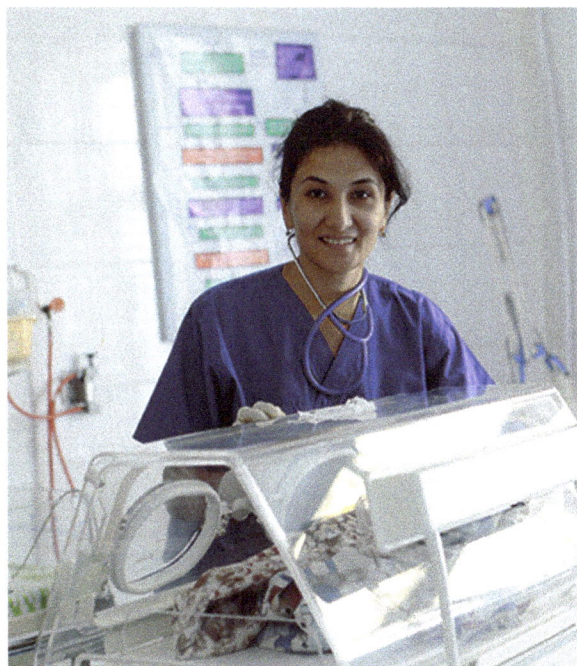

The project helped upgrade the curriculum for nurses and doctors to international standards.

> "The ADB project has contributed to a policy change in maternal and child health in line with the WHO recommendations... The improvement of the obstetric service became the foundation for the organization of perinatal centers and the regionalization of perinatal care in the republic.
>
> **—Asomidin Kamilov, former deputy minister of health, Uzbekistan**

Hashtags:
#Uzbekistan, #WomanAndChildCare, #Health, #HealthDevelopment, #WomenEmpowerment

Find out more:
- https://bit.ly/3AGQIUw
- https://bit.ly/3lGUof2
- https://bit.ly/3mSrzMk
- https://bit.ly/3iYOGUf

Making Health Care More Cost Effective and Available in Bangladesh

Project Name:	Secondary Urban Primary Health Care Project
Region/Country:	South Asia/Bangladesh
Sector and Themes:	Health
Year:	2005
Project Leader:	Brian Chin

> *The proportion of women from the slums coming to the center for delivery and other health care services has doubled to more than 70% in the last few years.*
>
> **—Kazi Nurun Nabi, physician and program director, Al-Haj Jahurul Islam Matri Sadan Maternity Center**

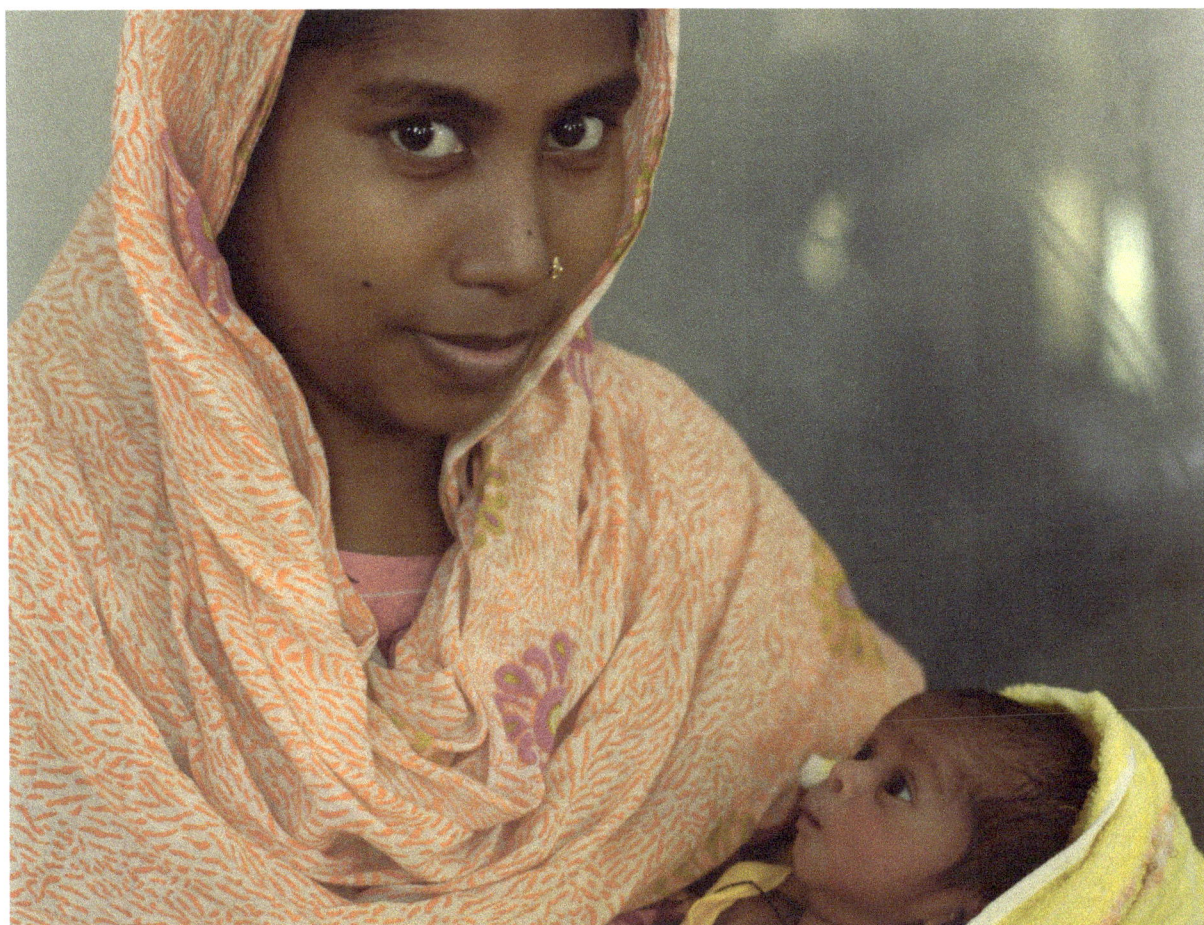

Urban primary health care was a neglected sector in Bangladesh.

Development challenge

Until recently, urban primary health care was a neglected sector in Bangladesh relative to other South Asian countries. Health indicators of the urban poor were declining and were sometimes even worse than those of the rural poor.

Solution

The Secondary Urban Primary Urban Health Care Project sought to make public health care services more available and cost effective to the urban poor, especially by reducing child and maternal mortality and morbidity. The project aimed to increase use of urban primary health care services; improve the quality of urban primary care services in the project area; and improve the cost-effectiveness, efficiency,

and institutional and financial sustainability of primary care to meet the needs of the urban poor.

The project achieved this by building reproductive and primary health care centers to provide maternal and child care to poor urban communities. Each reproductive health care center was staffed with an ambulance service and employed 32 staff, including a physician, a pediatrician, and four medical officers. The primary health care centers have 10 staff. A special feature of the project was the contracting of primary health care services to 12 nongovernment organizations (NGOs) through 24 partnerships between the NGOs and city corporations and municipalities. The partner NGOs provided essential services including HIV and sexually transmitted infection control and supplementary nutrition.

Knowledge products and services delivered

The project focused on the provision of primary health care through partner NGOs. Emphasis was placed on behavioral change communication and marketing, and on building capacity and policy support for urban primary care. The project supported involvement of beneficiaries, health staff, and government officials in the preparatory stage. It trained nearly 3,000 people, half of whom were women, in clinical or management aspects. The project specifically targeted women and young children.

Impact and results

The project brought about a change in mindset and lifestyle. The project had a target population of 9.41 million, approximately 23% of the urban population of Bangladesh. From 2005 to 2012, 10.22 million individual clients attended project-supported clinics, of whom 78% were female. Overall, the project saw an increase in cumulative service contacts as well as increase in utilization among the poor.

Lessons learned

Public–private partnerships for primary health service delivery among the urban poor, and particularly women and children, proved to be a replicable, effective, and innovative approach. Pro-poor targeting proved difficult without necessary and adequate provisions and safeguards in the bidding process for selection of partner agencies. Efficient cash and fund flows were essential for the smooth operation of the private partner agencies.

Through behavioral change communications, marketing, capacity building and policy support, the project brought about a change in mindset and lifestyle with regard to urban primary health care.

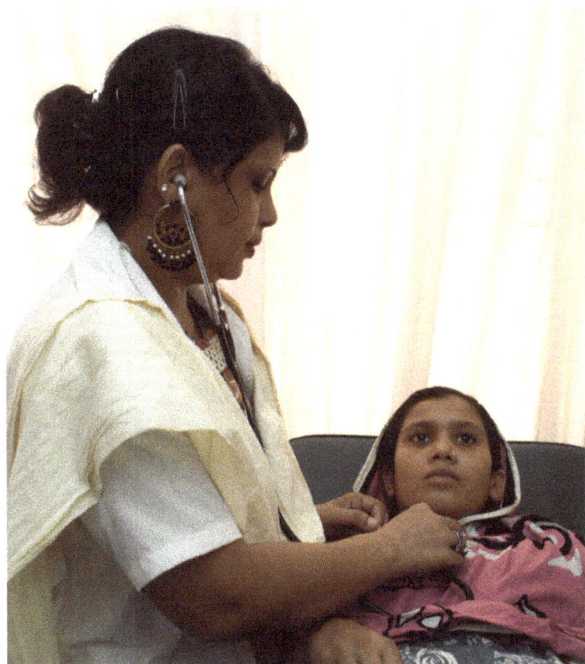

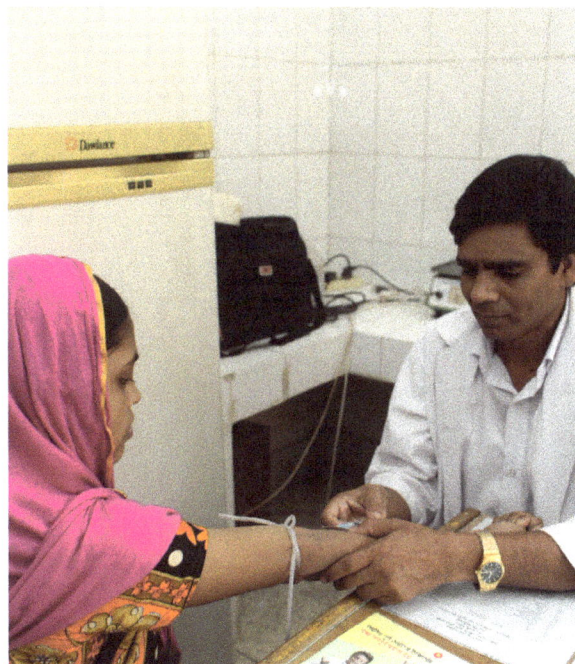

Public–private partnerships proved to be effective and innovative in primary health service delivery among urban poor, especially women and children.

"

We believe our health centers have contributed to a substantial reduction in maternal deaths in Bangladesh.

—Kazi Nurun Nabi, project manager, Progoti Samaj Kallyan Protisthan, an NGO operating health care centers in Dhaka

Hashtags:
#Healthcare, #Bangladesh, #DiseasePrevention, #HealthSector

Find out more:
- https://bit.ly/3j3PbME
- https://bit.ly/3j05H03
- https://bit.ly/3FIdgCB
- https://bit.ly/3BVFWFC

Improving HIV Prevention in the Greater Mekong Subregion

Project Name:	Greater Mekong Subregion Capacity Building for HIV/AIDS Prevention Project
Region/Countries:	Southeast Asia/Viet Nam and Lao People's Democratic Republic
Sector and Themes:	Health
Year:	2012–2018
Project Leader:	Ye Xu

The project focused on regional dialogue and information exchange that can be used in the planning of HIV/AIDS services at the national and subnational levels.

ADB project team with frontline staff from methadone treatment facility in Viet Nam.

Development challenge

Rapid economic development in the Greater Mekong Subregion has increased the movement of people and goods, resulting in greater vulnerability to HIV. There are particular challenges to addressing the HIV epidemic in the subregion. In 2011, Viet Nam was aiming for nationwide HIV prevention, treatment, and care, focusing on high-risk populations in major cities and in border districts. In the Lao People's Democratic Republic (Lao PDR), increased mobility across border districts and the commercial sex trade created a high-risk environment. The AIDS response was inefficient due to limited staff capacity, and inadequate access to quality prevention and care services. Awareness of the risks of HIV was low among high-risk and vulnerable populations, including migrants and mobile individuals. A concerted new effort was needed to expand HIV awareness and reduce HIV prevalence.

Solution

ADB designed a loan and a project preparatory TA for the governments of the Lao PDR and Viet Nam in consultation with their respective ministries of health and major stakeholder groups to strengthen awareness on HIV. The TA (funded by the Japan Fund for Poverty Reduction) and loan targeted capacity building of government departments and frontline staff through technical training programs.

The project also upgraded facilities and provided equipment for HIV programs. Behavior change communication activities spread mass awareness to target populations with increased risk. The two countries signed an MOU on a joint strategy for regional cooperation and cross-border collaboration. ADB provided block grant mechanisms, piloted in the Lao PDR, for innovative HIV service delivery models targeting migrants, mobile populations, and other high-risk groups at border areas.

Knowledge products and services delivered

The TA prioritized stakeholder participation, ownership, and careful selection of project sites and scope of activities to complement the support provided by other development partners. The TA supplemented the project loan to build the capacities of the national HIV/AIDS committees, program staff, and health managers. It supported private practitioners to manage sexually transmitted infections and to provide voluntary counseling and testing services, and trained peer educators and

village health workers in community-based behavior change communication activities. It developed training materials and toolkits for developing the HIV prevention and control plan, which were integrated in the annual operational plans of respective provincial health departments. The project produced seven border province profiles and five case studies capturing the practical experience and impacts of the interventions and organized regional and national learning events.

Impact and results

The project increased knowledge in HIV transmission and means of prevention. It improved coordination with the respective national HIV/AIDS prevention programs. Both countries were able to update their national guidelines and standard operating procedures for comprehensive delivery of HIV prevention services that complemented the establishment of anti-retroviral therapy centers.

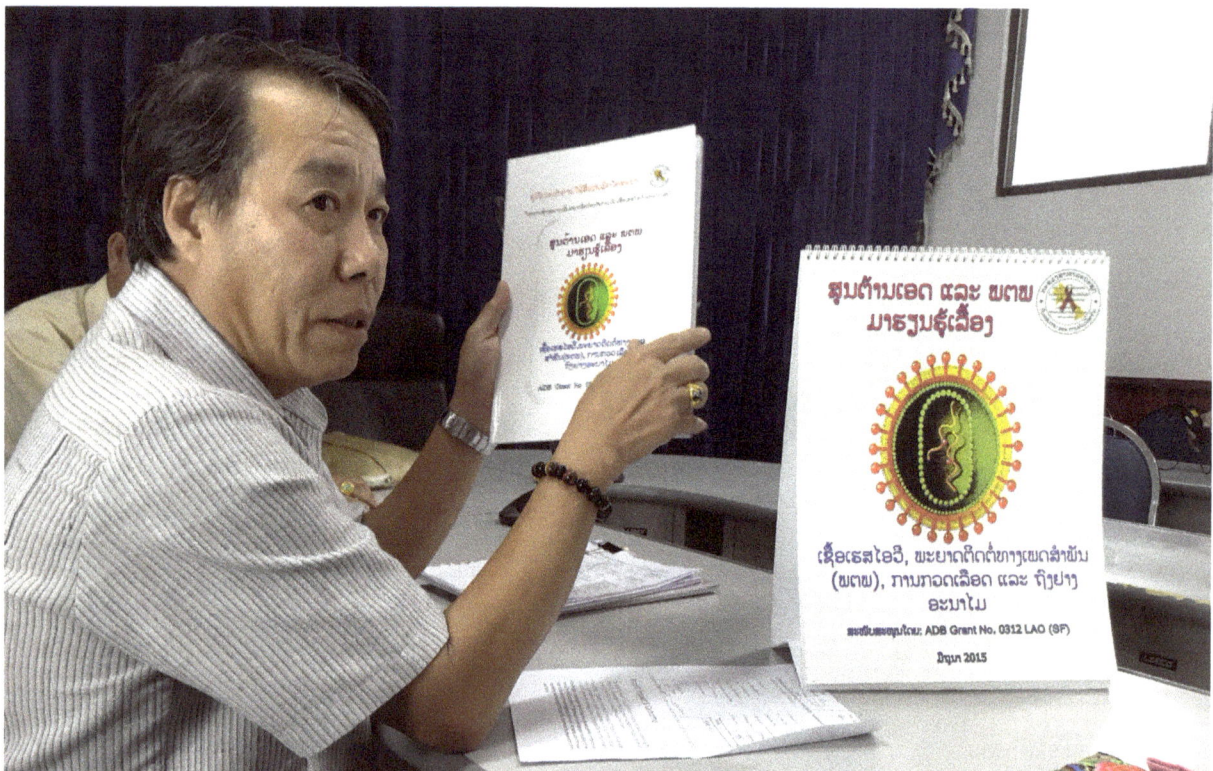

The project increased knowledge in HIV transmission and means of prevention.

The project supported cross-country coordination and collaboration, focusing on strengthening cooperation and knowledge exchange on HIV response at border areas and communities.

Lessons for replication

The project focused on regional cooperation, through dialogue and information exchange that can be localized in the national and subnational planning of HIV/AIDS services. If block grants are to be employed, the project's institutional context and fund flow mechanisms should be considered to ensure executing agencies can engage NGOs for project interventions in hard-to-reach populations. The project also offers important lessons for communication strategies that have widespread impact on HIV prevention messaging.

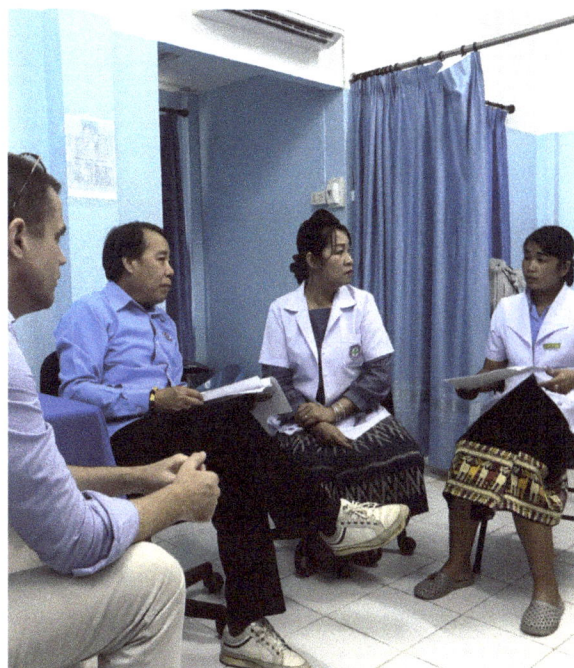

The project supported strengthening of cooperation and knowledge exchange on HIV response at border areas and communities.

> *Now I know about sexual health issues. If we are not cautious, we may get HIV.*
>
> **—"Buntheon," entertainment worker, Cambodia**

Hashtags:
#Prevention, #Healthcare, #LaoPDR, #VietNam, #HIVAids, #CapacityBuilding, #Knowledge, #RegionalCooperation

Find out more:
- https://bit.ly/3mTN7YS

Supporting Vaccination by Increasing Health System Resilience in the Pacific

Project Name: System Strengthening for Effective Coverage of New Vaccines in the Pacific Project

Region/Countries: Pacific/Samoa, Tonga, Tuvalu, and Vanuatu

Sector and Themes: Health

Year: 2017–Present

Project Leader: Inez Mikkelsen-Lopez

> *We want to empower women and others. We want to give them the knowledge they need to understand and appreciate how important vaccines are.*
> **—Karlos Lee Moresi, chief executive officer,**
> **Ministry of Health, Tuvalu**

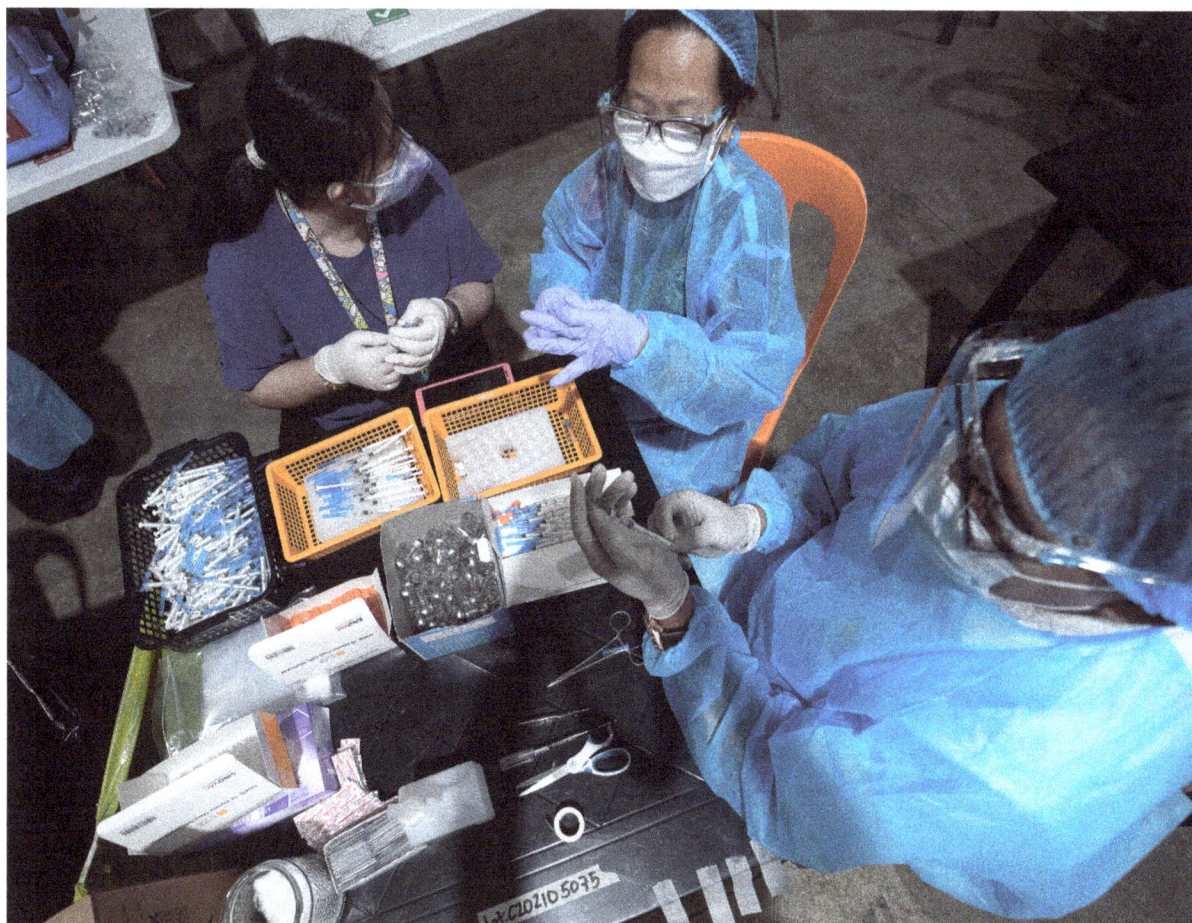

The project forms part of the regional response to reduce the number of cervical cancer cases and other infectious diseases in children and women.

Development challenge

The Pacific region especially has a high incidence of cervical cancer, pneumonia, and diarrhea—all of which are easily preventable through vaccines. Cervical cancer resulted in 500 premature deaths in the Pacific region in 2010 alone. Pneumonia and diarrhea together take the lives of 3 out of 10 children under the age of 5 in the Pacific islands.

Samoa, Tonga, Tuvalu, and Vanuatu do not have vaccination programs to tackle these diseases. Their health systems, with limited capacity in diagnostic and specialist services, impedes early screening and treatment. They are disadvantaged by outdated equipment, shortages of skilled staff, and issues of last-mile connectivity. The countries need well-designed immunization programs that can be delivered through resilient local health systems.

Solution

ADB worked closely with the ministries of finance and health of these nations to procure three quality-assured vaccines through the United Nations Children's Fund (UNICEF) global medical procurement scheme: HPV vaccine for cervical cancer, pneumococcal conjugate vaccine for pneumonia, and rotavirus vaccine for diarrhea. The project acquired cold chain equipment and associated supplies from UNICEF to strengthen vaccine delivery infrastructure. At the local level, the project ensured vaccine microplanning at 90% of health facilities.

The project promoted health system resilience and equity through immunization and cold chain management guidelines, and capacity building of health workers in vaccine planning, administration, data reporting, and waste management. Quality and equity of vaccine management was checked through data on sex-disaggregated immunization reporting and evidence from nationwide immunization and health surveys. A bottom-up community-based approach was used, which leveraged existing community structures and communication channels.

Knowledge products and services delivered

Apart from procuring vaccines and vaccine-related infrastructure, the project facilitated capacity building of health staff through training programs and workshops and introduced best practices in immunization and vaccine delivery to ensure equitable vaccine distribution. Community awareness programs with a focus on women improved the population's attitude toward vaccines. Sex-disaggregated immunization reporting and evidence from nationwide health surveys were used to ensure quality and equity of the immunization programs.

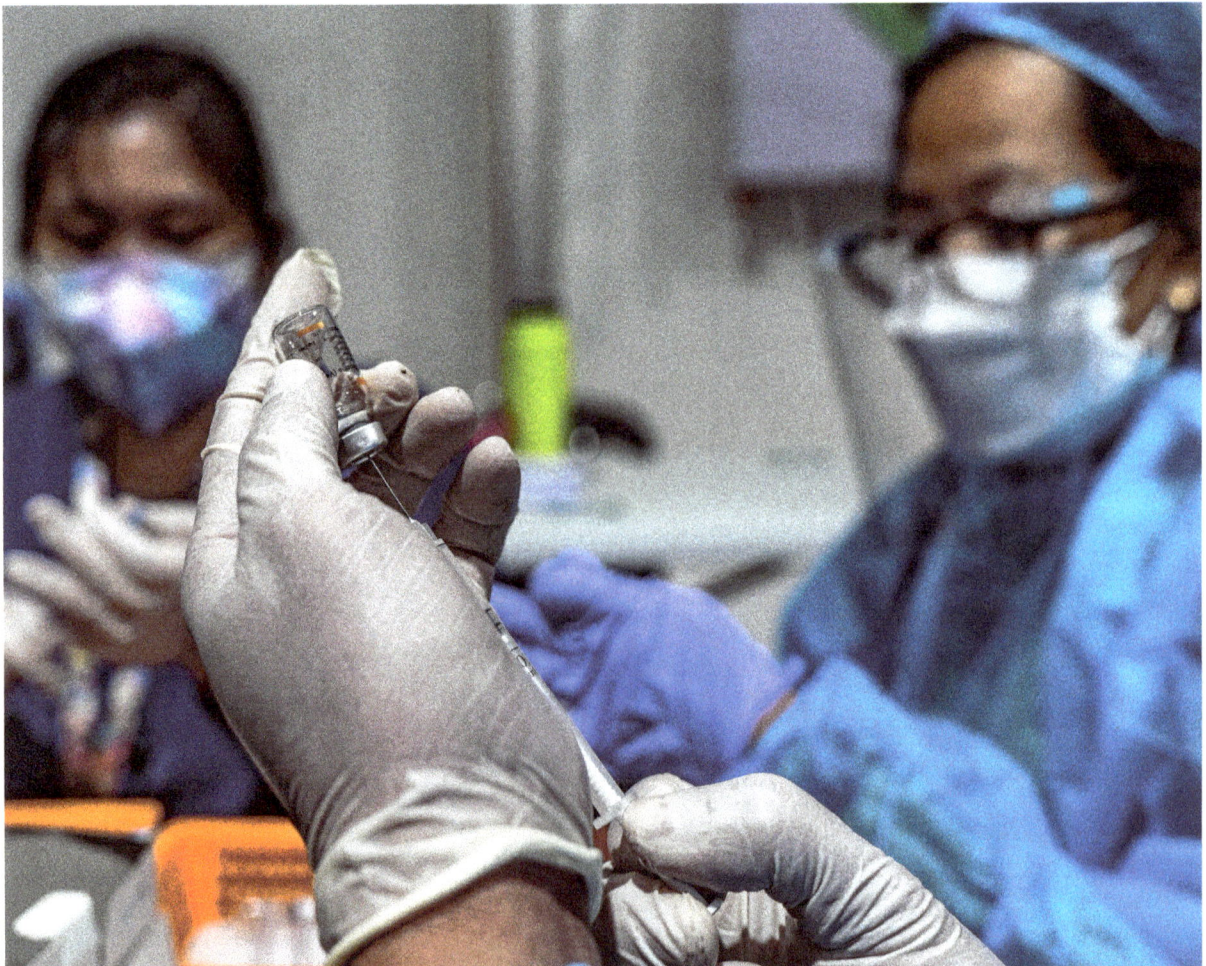

The project uses the introduction of new vaccines and early detection through communicable disease platforms to drive necessary improvements in the public health system in selected Pacific developing member countries.

Impact and results

The project will protect more than 580,000 young women and children against cervical cancer, pneumonia, and diarrhea. The project has received widespread, enthusiastic support from the participating countries and UNICEF.

Lessons for replication

The project highlights the importance of increasing resilience of health systems to tackle such diseases through health facilities and capacity building. Guidelines and processes established for immunization, cold chain management, and capacity building could serve as a helpful resource for other countries tackling HPV, pneumonia, and rotavirus. Sex-disaggregated immunization data collection creates an invaluable dataset for quantitative policy research on vaccination.

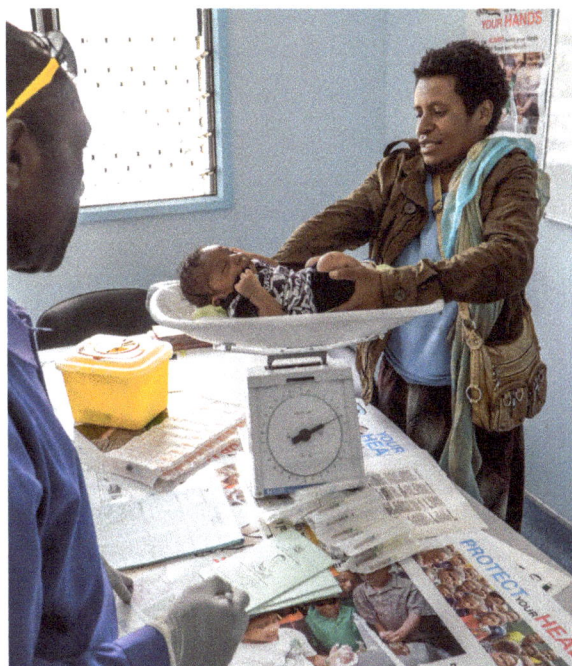

The rollout of vaccines to protect children against cervical cancer, pneumonia, and rotavirus has begun in several Pacific developing member countries.

> *The consequences of the recent measles epidemic in Samoa have highlighted the need to strengthen immunization programs in the country.*
> **—Take Naseri, director general, Ministry of Health, Samoa**

Hashtags:

#Prevention, #Healthcare, #LaoPDR, #VietNam, #HIVAids, #CapacityBuilding, #Knowledge, #RegionalCooperation

Find out more:
- https://bit.ly/3aDteiO
- https://bit.ly/30jGreQ
- https://bit.ly/3j3Pze4
- https://bit.ly/3FOAdnC
- https://bit.ly/3mSGpIT

Achieving Universal Health Coverage in Asia and the Pacific

Project Name:	Asian Development Bank–Japan International Cooperation Agency Meeting on Achieving Universal Health Coverage in Asia and the Pacific
Region/Country:	Japan
Sector and Themes:	Health
Year:	2019
Project Leaders:	Takehiko Nakao and Kitaoka Shinichi

"Sharing all of our experiences and lessons, whether successful or unsuccessful, is one of our responsibilities in this region to advance UHC.

—Shinichi Kitaoka, president, Japan International Cooperation Agency

ADB Social Development Thematic Group Chief Wendy Walker moderating the session on Emerging Opportunities to Achieve Universal Health Coverage in Asia during the ADB-JICA Meeting on Achieving Universal Health Coverage in Asia and the Pacific held in Tokyo, Japan, in February 2019.

Development challenge

Asia and the Pacific, home to more than half of the world's population, continues to face barriers to achieving universal health coverage (UHC)— that is, equitable access to quality health care without undue financial burden. These include communicable diseases, aging, and income disparity between the rich and the poor. Artemisinin-resistant malaria is a continuing challenge in the region. Other communicable diseases also do not respect national borders. A few countries still experience wild poliovirus transmission. The working-age population in Asia and the Pacific also continues to shrink as populations undergo drastic aging.

The burden of noncommunicable diseases has become more serious because elderly populations are more susceptible to illness. Income disparities between the rich and the poor have also been aggravated by the disproportionate financial burden of ill-health on poor families.

Solution

Achieving UHC contributes to equitable economic growth while stabilizing societies and making them more climate resilient. In support of this, ADB and the Japan International Cooperation Agency (JICA) organized a meeting during the G20 Summit to jointly agree on concrete outcomes for UHC, keeping a climate-resilient lens.

Knowledge products and services delivered

The TA supported the ADB–JICA joint summit on 13 February 2019 in Tokyo that also served as an input to the G20 Summit in Osaka in June 2019. The meeting came to some important conclusions. While domestic financing was identified as the primary revenue source for UHC, it must be complemented by innovative financing solutions. Blended financing (combining loans, grants, and TA) could fast-track progress toward UHC. The meeting participants called for collaborative efforts across stakeholders, including WHO, the Global Fund, GAVI (Gavi, The Vaccine Alliance), multilateral development banks, ministries of finance and health, and international and local NGOs.

Impact and results

The event enabled participants to discover new approaches for sustainable health financing to ensure UHC. It provided fresh perspectives on financing to achieve UHC as part of the SDG agenda. It also strengthened the ADB–JICA partnership and reinforced the joint MOU that was signed in May 2017 to establish a strategic partnership to strengthen health security and promote UHC in a rapidly aging Asia and Pacific region. The meeting provided vital inputs for the G20 Summit in Osaka, which took UHC as a major theme.

The event enabled participants to discover new approaches for sustainable health financing to ensure universal health care.

> "
> *Under our new long-term Strategy 2030, in response to Asia and the Pacific's growing needs for health services, ADB is scaling up our health sector operations with a focus on UHC.*
> **—Takehiko Nakao, former president, ADB**

Lessons for replication

As countries continue to grapple with the COVID-19 pandemic, achieving UHC plays a vital role in recovery and in building communities that are resilient to future health risks. The current crisis presents an opportunity to take stock of ADB's own programs, and joint initiatives to promote UHC. Similar future events can examine the lessons learned from managing projects during a pandemic, especially the role that ADB can play when collaborating with development partners.

The meeting provided vital inputs for the G20 Summit in Osaka, which took universal health care as a major theme.

Hashtags:
#UniversalHealthCoverage, #UHC, #Health, #HealthFinancing, #Collaboration, #Strategy2030 #SDG

Bringing Law and Policy Reform Where it is Needed

Project Name:	Institutionalization of Office of the General Counsel's Law and Policy Reform Program
Region/Country:	Regional/All Developing Member Countries
Sector and Themes:	Governance and Public Sector Management
Year:	2020
Project Leader:	Christina Pak

Good governance, in particular, the rule of law and legal and judicial institutions, is vital to inclusive and sustainable development.

Republic of Fiji Solicitor General Sharvada Sharma welcoming participants to the inaugural Pacific Regional International Arbitration Conference held in Denarau Island, Nadi, Fiji, in February 2018.

Development challenge

Every year, millions of jobs and billions of dollars of economic activity are at risk because of the absence of a strong legal framework in ADB's DMCs. Investment in sectors such as infrastructure, energy, manufacturing, and tourism depends on the stability of a country's policies and laws, without which unsustainable economic activity can have long-lasting impacts on the environment and biodiversity. For gender inequality and gender-based violence, legal recourse is sometimes the only option.

Solution

The Office of the General Counsel (OGC) has been managing ADB's Law and Policy Reform Program since 1995, where OGC designs and implements

TA projects in areas relating to legal and judicial reforms. The Law and Policy Reform Program team has expertise in environment and climate change, private sector development, infrastructure law and regulation, financial law and regulation, and inclusive growth (including gender equality) and access to justice.

Knowledge products and services delivered

In 2019, OGC developed a Law and Policy Reform Program action plan. It provides law and policy reform services, identifying legal barriers before projects or investments are initiated. It also provides design and implementation support to policy-based program and TA operations. To deliver more law and policy reform services, OGC realigned its internal structure based on a "hub and spokes" model, where a newly formed law and policy reform team will act as the hub, and OGC lawyers from the different teams act as spokes providing their knowledge and expertise. OGC put in place internal measures to strengthen governance, quality assurance, and business processes for improved law and policy reform services.

Impact and results

The Law and Policy Reform Program has improved the legal and regulatory frameworks and capacities of legal and judicial stakeholders in ADB's DMCs. Highlights include legal reforms to attract foreign investment and support private sector development and public–private partnerships (PPPs) in Pacific DMCs, Timor-Leste, and Uzbekistan. The program created a legal framework for international arbitration so that commercial disputes between foreign parties can be effectively resolved and enforced.

The program helped enact a new PPP law in Viet Nam in June 2020 to replace the existing decree. The new law increases overall transparency, provides stronger government support for PPP development, reduces long-term risks, and makes it more attractive for private sector commitments. In the Lao PDR, the program helped the government enact a new disaster management law, which sets out roles and responsibilities and coordinating mechanisms for the central and provincial level entities involved in the disaster response and recovery effort.

The conference secretariat, which includes ADB Principal Counsel Christina Pak, together with speakers at the conference.

Lessons for replication

Law and policy reform conversations need to occur early on during drafting of country partnership strategies and country programming missions. They also need to be integrated into work plans of the sector and thematic groups. ADB can leverage the program's operational knowledge, subject matter expertise, and long-term relationships with legal and judicial stakeholders to deliver more law and policy reform solutions.

One of the sessions in the Pacific Regional International Arbitration Conference.

Hashtags:
#OGC, #Law, #Policy, #Regulation, #LegalFramework

Find out more:
- https://bit.ly/3BQfldq

Fostering Gender Inclusivity Through Evidence-Based Policy Making in the Pacific

Project Name:	Promoting Evidence-Based Policy Making for Gender Equality in the Pacific
Region/Country:	Pacific
Sector:	Governance and Public Sector Management
Year:	2010–2015
Project Leader:	Sunhwa Lee

The project produced comprehensive country gender assessments based on rigorous empirical analyses and regional gender statistics, both of which were much needed for the Pacific DMCs.

In many Pacific countries, persistent gender gaps in enrollment rates is a critical concern.

Development challenge

Many Pacific countries rank low in the human and gender-related development indicators of the United Nations Development Programme, including basic health and education outcomes, particularly among women. Persistent gender gaps in enrollment rates, high maternal mortality rates, lack of women empowerment, low participation of women in the economy and decision-making positions, along with widespread gender-based violence, are critical concerns for improving women's status. Weak technical capacity across government agencies in Pacific DMCs has constrained systematic and concerted policy efforts to address such gender concerns.

Solution

ADB approved a regional TA project in 2010 to assess gender-related barriers in selected Pacific DMCs and to build governments' capacity in systematic monitoring of progress and challenges in gender equality. The project targeted women's ministries and national statistical agencies. The project supported Cook Islands, Fiji, Marshall Islands, Papua New Guinea, Solomon Islands, Timor-Leste, Tonga, and Vanuatu. Staff from the respective women's ministries and national statistics offices from each of these countries participated.

Inputs from multiple government representatives from different ministries also enhanced understanding of specific gender-related challenges across various sectors. Civil society and development partners also helped build a broader consensus approach to regional gender issues across Pacific DMCs. The results indicated a continuous need to improve gender awareness across Pacific governments and develop institutional and technical capacities of government agencies to promote evidence-based policy making on gender equity.

Knowledge products and services delivered

Comprehensive country gender assessments were produced in Fiji, Papua New Guinea (with World Bank and other development partners), Solomon Islands, and Timor-Leste (with the United Nations Development Fund for Women), while Cook Islands, Marshall Islands, and Tonga received additional capacity building. The four assessments were published as government-led documents in collaboration with other development partners and involving extensive outreach. *Gender Statistics*,[28] was published in 2016, demonstrating ADB's significant value addition in the Pacific and Timor-Leste to promote evidence-based monitoring and policy making on gender equality. The publication was produced in collaboration with the Secretariat of the Pacific Community, and its findings disseminated in several regional workshops.

Impact and results

The project produced comprehensive country gender assessments. The TA helped build the capacity of key government agencies, especially

Civil society and development partners helped build a broader consensus approach to regional gender issues across Pacific developing member countries.

---

[28] ADB. 2016. *Gender Statistics for the Pacific and Timor-Leste.* Manila.

national statistics offices, women's sector offices, and sector gender focal points for evidence-based policy making on gender issues. The TA raised awareness on the importance of gender statistics, which could be powerful in advancing essential gender equality agenda. The gender awareness and statistical training helped the Pacific DMCs develop more credible gender action plans and gender monitoring. A follow-on TA is continuing his work toward gender mainstreaming across health ministries and departments, and in building capacities to conduct country gender assessments in smaller countries.

The TA helped build the capacity of women's sector offices, and sector gender focal points, among others, for evidence-based policy making on gender issues.

Lessons for replication

The country gender assessment process required strong technical and research capacities, as well as extensive consultation efforts. For smaller countries, it may be more useful to do an abbreviated version. Building broader political consensus across various sector agencies from earlier on will help in identifying specific sector-based gender issues and developing effective gender mainstreaming strategies. ADB's strong leadership in advocating evidence-based policy making and building collaboration networks with development partners was essential for the successful outcome of this TA.

"

ADB's highlighted the importance of gender advocacy, equipped with monitoring gender indicators. This is essential for creating convincing messages across different sectors and building sustained efforts toward gender equality."

—Sunhwa Lee, principal social sector specialist, Human and Social Development Division, South Asia Department, ADB

Hashtags:
#Gender, #WomenEmpowerment, #GenderMainstreaming, #GenderAwareness #Statistics, #PolicyMaking

Innovative Value-Capture Financing Mechanism and Functioning Cities for Achieving Sustainable Urbanization

Project Name: The Urbanization–Poverty–Inequality Triangle in Asia and the Pacific

Region/Country: Regional/All Developing Member Countries

Sector and Themes: Governance and Public Sector Management

Year: 2013

Project Leader: Jiang Yi

"*To function as a vibrant job market, cities need affordable and efficient public transport that is well regulated.*
—Yasuyuki Sawada, chief economist, ADB"

A collaborative effort led by several ADB regional and thematic departments helped in understanding the complex urbanization–poverty–inequality triangle. In the photo is ADB Vice-President Bambang Susantono and delegates in the High-Level Round Table Discussion held in Bangkok, Thailand in May 2019.

Development challenge

ADB estimates[29] that urbanization plans will cost $1.7 trillion between 2016 and 2030.[30] They will require innovative funding mechanisms for the necessary infrastructure projects. Value capture is one such mechanism that has great potential to provide governments with substantial revenues to fund their ambitious objectives. It aims to identify comprehensive benefits of infrastructure investment projects and find mechanisms so that beneficiaries contribute proportionately to the funding of the investments. To support these funding needs, ADB needs to bolster its understanding of the relationship between urbanization, poverty, and inequality; and increase its capacity to implement mechanisms like land value capture to help DMCs fund sustainable plans.

Solution

A collaborative effort led by several ADB regional and thematic departments helped in understanding the complex urbanization–poverty–inequality triangle. Research by ADB and ADBI culminated in a deeper appreciation for the potential of land value capture as an innovative funding mechanism for infrastructure projects. The project worked with universities and think tanks to provide evidence-based case studies and quantitative research solutions to highlight the potential of this approach and provide steps for its implementation in big cities.

[29] ADB. 2017. *Meeting Asia's Infrastructure Needs*. Manila.
[30] The technical assistance was originally initiated by economists in the then Development Indicators and Policy Research Division of the Economic Research and Regional Cooperation Department (ERCD). After reorganization in 2019, the administration and implementation of the technical assistance was transferred to the Economic Analysis and Operational Support Division of ERCD.

Knowledge products and services delivered

The project supported datasets in infrastructure financing. A database built on novel geo-referenced urban data spanned 43 economies from the Asia and Pacific region. It used satellite-based remote sensing data from 1992 to 2016, providing valuable data for research on urbanization. It collected shape, area, population, and city characteristics covering 1,500 cities in these economies. Another database collated detailed trip data from Google Maps in selected Asian cities to obtain up-to-date measures and understanding of congestion across major cities in the region.

The project produced several evidence-based reports including Sustaining Transit Investment in Asia's Cities: A Beneficiary-Funding and Land Value Capture Perspective.[31] The report provided quantitative analysis on the potential for land value capture and presented steps to implement this in megacities like Bangkok, Jakarta, and Manila. It also generated 32 background papers and 10 research papers on the urbanization–poverty–inequality triangle and value-capture financing, which were widely disseminated through workshops and conferences with the DMCs.

Impact and results

Research on urbanization-related topics has led to policy dialogue and work on urbanization–growth issues. The Government of Indonesia has included land value capture as a funding mechanism for public investment projects in its National Medium-Term Development Planning 2020–2024 and has requested ADB's advice on this. An ongoing project in coordination with NITI Aayog, the premier policy think tank of the Government of India, is sensitizing state governments on urbanization issues as they relate to growth and economic opportunities

Lessons for replication

This project provides a template for countries to design and implement land value capture to fund infrastructure projects by increasing government revenues. The project can also inform development of city-related geo-referenced databases, which can be a valuable resource for research and policy making. The project highlighted the importance of active stakeholder engagement and participation at every stage.

The project generated background papers and research papers on the urbanization–poverty–inequality triangle and value-capture financing, which were widely disseminated through workshops and conferences.

---

[31]   ADB. 2019. *Sustaining Transit Investment in Asia's Cities: A Beneficiary-Funding and Land Value Capture Perspective.* Manila.

"

Adopting land value capture in cities like Jakarta, Bangkok, and Manila creates a triple win. The first win is that it helps finance metro systems and thus improves overall urban mobility. The second win is that if used properly, it reduces the subsidy levels required in running metro systems, since the money can also go toward operating costs. For the third win, the money generated from land value capture creates the fiscal space to use government finance productively for other sectors—such as health, education, and slum improvement.

—Bambang Susantono, vice-president for knowledge management and sustainable development, ADB

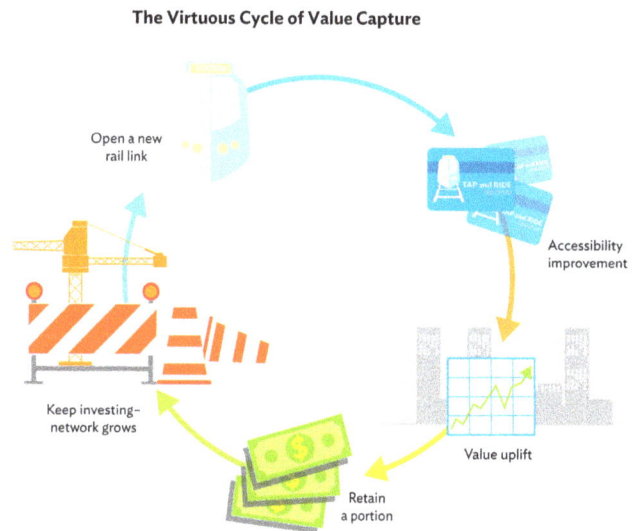

The Virtuous Cycle of Value Capture

Open a new rail link

Accessibility improvement

Value uplift

Retain a portion

Keep investing– network grows

Hashtags:

#Regional, #Urbanization, #Poverty, #Inequality, #InfrastructureFinancing, #ValueCapture #LandValueCapture

Find out more:

- https://bit.ly/3BF2uui
- https://bit.ly/3BKCOfW
- https://bit.ly/3IJTJtA
- https://bit.ly/3aFwcU4
- https://bit.ly/3p49aPI

Future-Proofing Nauru through Fiscal Sustainability

Project Name:	Fiscal Sustainability Reform Program
Region/Country:	Pacific/Nauru
Sector and Themes:	Governance and Public Sector Management
Year:	2015–2017
Project Leaders:	Hayden Everett, Liliana Warid, and He Rong

" *A stronger funding mechanism for future service delivery through the Nauru Intergenerational Trust Fund is one of the program's latest major achievements.*

—**David Adeang, former minister of finance, Nauru** "

Nauru's economy depends primarily on phosphate deposits and the oceanic resources of its exclusive economic zone.

Development challenge

Nauru is ADB's smallest member country with a population of approximately 10,800 people. Most of its economy depends primarily on phosphate deposits and the oceanic resources of its exclusive economic zone. The public sector dominates the economy. The civil service and state-owned enterprises (SOEs), particularly the Nauru Utilities Corporation (NUC), accounted for 82% of total employment in 2010.

However, Nauru's public sector has weak institutional capacity and faces many infrastructure

bottlenecks. This dependence on a narrow set of uncertain revenue streams, coupled with weak infrastructure and institutions, raises crucial questions on Nauru's long-term financial and macroeconomic stability.

Solution

With cofinancing from Australia, ADB worked closely with Nauru's Ministry of Finance and NUC to promote fiscal sustainability. The program improved Nauru's public financial management capabilities by establishing expenditure controls, cash management practices, and designing and implementing a financial management information system. To increase revenues, an Employment and Services Tax bill was drafted and implemented. Future revenues and expenditures were also projected for the first time in Nauru. Apart from public financial management improvements, the project actively sought to resolve infrastructure bottlenecks by strengthening NUC's performance and service delivery. A business strategy plan for the corporation and a maintenance plan for its assets were key in further commercialization of the SOE.

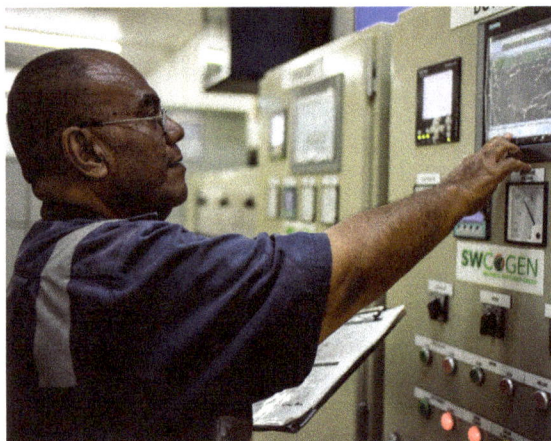

The project actively sought to resolve infrastructure bottlenecks by strengthening NUC's performance and service delivery.

One of the most important components for future fiscal sustainability was the program's support in establishing a trust fund to efficiently save windfall revenues and fiscally future-proof Nauru.

Knowledge products and services delivered

A financial management information system, rolled out for the entire government, incorporated projecting future revenues and expenditure. From September 2014, when the Employment and Services Tax bill was passed, to June 2015, the tax generated A\$6.6 million (\$5.1 million) in revenue, while A\$12.6 million (\$9.8 million) was generated in the 2016 financial year. A business strategy plan and an asset maintenance plan were designed and implemented to improve NUC's performance and service. This included a performance management system for all employees, financial accounting software, and an asset rehabilitation plan to upgrade the power network. The Nauru Intergenerational Trust Fund was also established between Nauru and Australia to fund Nauru's future financial requirements.

Impact and results

The financial management information system produced the first financial statement of the government since 1995. In 2015, aggregate revenue and expenditure projections for the 2016–2018 financial years enabled the government to forecast budgets and improve investment strategies. The NUC's asset maintenance plan has significantly improved operating efficiency, and an informed approach to setting tariffs.

> "
> *This [project] reformed our work culture and improved our processes... It was one of the ways we were able to put the Nauru Utilities Corporation on a path toward financial sustainability.*
> —**Abraham Simpson, chief executive officer, Nauru Utilities Corporation**

The Nauru Intergenerational Trust Fund has succeeded in pulling together A$33.4 million ($25.9 million), including A$20.4 million ($15.8 million) from the government, and the remainder from Australia and Taipei,China.

Lessons for replication

This project provides valuable insights on developing and implementing successful financial management software. Projects concerned with SOE reforms could look at how the NUC was commercialized and how its financial and operating performance was improved through a comprehensive business strategy and asset management strategy. Other countries that are fiscally constrained with limited and volatile sources of revenue could study how an intergenerational fund can be set up with international partners to financially future-proof their countries.

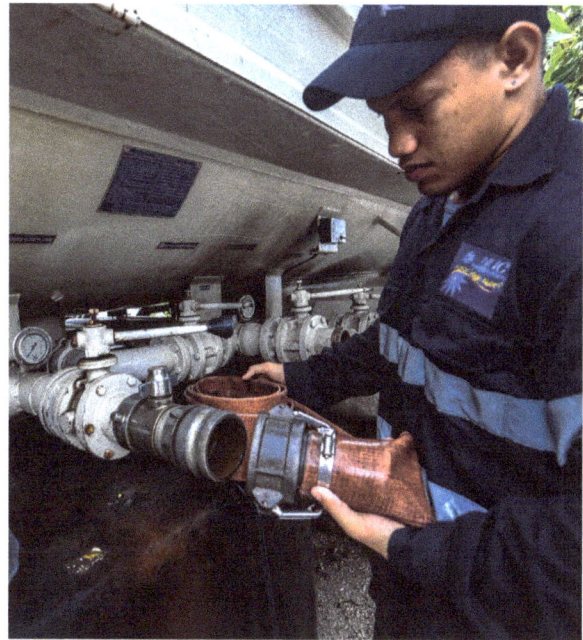

The program will help the Government of Nauru deliver improved social services.

> *Life has changed for the better... There are far fewer power cuts now.*
> **—Beniana Foilape, resident, Boe District**

Hashtags:

#Nauru, #FiscalReforms, #IntergenerationalFund, #PublicFinancialManagement #FiscalSustainability, #Pacific

Find out more:

- https://bit.ly/3DK2BFs
- https://bit.ly/3mYu0Na
- https://bit.ly/3p88b0m
- https://bit.ly/3j2VbWe

Supporting Disaster Resilience in the Pacific

Project Name: Pacific Disaster Resilience Program

Region/Country: Regional

Sector and Themes: Governance and Public Sector Management

Year: 2017–Present

Project Leader: Hanna Uusimaa

> " *The swift Pacific Disaster Resilience Program response set a good example. It motivated other development partners to speed up their funding and help for the government in the Cyclone Gita recovery.* "
>
> **—Pohiva Tu'i'onetoa, minister of finance and national planning, Tonga**

The program will improve the resilience of the participating countries to disasters triggered by natural hazards.

Development challenge

ADB's Pacific DMCs are highly exposed to different types of natural hazards. The region also experiences a disproportionately high share of global disaster impacts relative to its economic and demographic size. When disasters strike, countries in the Pacific face further challenges because their relatively small populations are dispersed over several islands that can be isolated and difficult to reach.

Most Pacific DMCs have limited resources and capacity to invest in disaster risk reduction, and to facilitate timely recovery and reconstruction after a

disaster. Disasters in Pacific DMCs can erode years of economic development gains. Delays in response and recovery exacerbate the indirect economic and social costs of disasters.

Solution

ADB set up a contingent financing program to provide more timely financing for response, early recovery, and reconstruction activities for disaster events caused by all types of natural hazards. The first phase of the regional program was approved in December 2017 for Samoa, Tonga, and Tuvalu. The policy-based loan and policy-based grant modality was used to agree on disaster resilience-related policy actions for each participating DMC. These policy actions were targeted at strengthening the resilience of institutions and communities. Related TA monitors progress toward achieving the governments' long-term disaster risk management goals.

Knowledge products and services delivered

The program's achievements include providing quick-disbursing and predictable sources of financing for disaster events and supported country-specific policy actions. It incentivized the strengthening of disaster risk management through the design of country-specific post-program partnership frameworks. In Samoa, Tonga, and Tuvalu, the project mapped a comprehensive inventory of hazards, exposures, and assets, and analyzed the status of post-disaster public financial

management capacity. It analyzed existing risk assessment data platforms using geographic information systems and recommended ways to boost regional data and information sharing for better investment decisions and planning.

Impact and results

The Pacific Disaster Resilience Program supported regional collaboration toward strengthened disaster risk management and disaster risk financing. It addressed risks pertaining to disaster events that would normally exhaust annual contingency budgets or emergency funds but may not be cost effectively covered by insurance. The program provided $6 million for Tonga Cyclone Relief in 2018 following Cyclone Gita, $3 million for Tuvalu Cyclone Relief in 2020 following tropical cyclone Tino, and $2.9 million to Samoa in response to the COVID-19 pandemic.

The program supports policy actions in disaster risk management, and provides participating ADB Pacific developing member countries with a source of contingent financing for timely disaster response, early recovery, and reconstruction activities.

Lessons for replication

The Pacific DMCs face similar challenges in disaster risk management and can benefit greatly from taking a regional approach. The Multi Hazard Disaster Risk Assessment in Tonga serves as a pilot for future similar assessments in other Pacific DMCs to inform resilient urban development and adaptation planning.

It also supports a collaborative multi-country mechanism to provide contingent financing in the event of disasters triggered by natural hazards.

> *Predictable, quick-disbursing finance to fill resource gaps after major disasters facilitates faster early recovery and reconstruction.*
>
> **—Hanna Uusimaa, climate change specialist, Pacific Department, ADB**

Hashtags:

#Disaster, #DisasterRiskManagement, #DisasterRiskFinancing, #Pacific, #Samoa, #Tonga, #Tuvalu #Resilience

Find out more:

• https://bit.ly/3AJmvyv

Gender-Responsive Budgeting for Fiji

Project Name:	Supporting Public Financial Management Reform
Region/Country:	Pacific/Fiji
Sector and Themes:	Governance and Public Sector Management
Year:	2018–Present
Project Leader:	Pamela Wyatt

Having moved to a mindset of gender-responsive budgeting, the Government of Fiji was able to address the immediate impacts of COVID-19.

The Government of Fiji recognizes the potential for better targeted expenditure to help reduce poverty.

Development challenge

Before the COVID-19 pandemic, almost 30% of Fiji's population were living in poverty, with more than 60% living in rural areas. The onset of the COVID-19 pandemic increased the risk of more people falling into poverty. With its reliance on public spending, the government recognizes the potential for better targeted expenditure to help reduce poverty. The government needed help in deciding which among the ongoing budget reforms should be prioritized that would result in real impact.

Solution

In 2019, Fiji became one of seven countries globally to pilot the PEFA Gender-Responsive Budgeting Assessment Report and receive the "PEFA check" of approval. In 2021, Fiji's Cabinet supported the introduction of gender-responsive budgeting through pilots run in two ministries. The pilots incorporated gender-responsive budgeting principles in budget submission templates and provided training and ongoing support through the budget process. This is a critical first step to enable the strategic allocation of resources for government priorities in future budgets.

Knowledge products and services delivered

ADB supported the government objectives through both direct TA and by support in achieving specific reforms that provide a gender-responsive business and investment climate. ADB supported the development of a methodology and training material, and delivery of training for staff of the Ministry of Economy and the Ministry of Women, Children and Poverty Alleviation. A Cabinet paper outlining the reasons for introducing gender-responsive budgeting, its principles and potential impact was an important way to engage the government and obtain its approval, endorsement, and commitment. This is vital to ensure that their ministries will embrace the changes. Training was then developed for the pilot ministries for possible future rollouts. The longer-term effect of the reforms will have a transformational impact on gender equality, women's economic empowerment, and women's access to resources and services.

Impact and results

Having moved to a mindset of gender-responsive budgeting, the government was able to address the immediate impacts of COVID-19. This was achieved by providing support for women-owned and women-led business; direct cash transfers to informal workers, including for microenterprises owned by women; and a guidance note on the gendered impacts of COVID-19 in Fiji.

The government established a COVID-19 Gender Working Group to act on the recommendations from the paper. To increase women's voices and access to services and resources, the government carried out actions to introduce gender-responsive budgeting. For example, the Ministry of Fisheries redesigned a training program for women to make it more inclusive.

Implementing the project will help promote fiscal discipline, the strategic allocation of resources, and efficient service delivery.

Lessons for replication

A clear plan is needed with pilots and there is an opportunity to learn and improve before expanding. It is possible to design small steps that make a start and can be built on. Successful ongoing implementation of gender-responsive budgeting reforms across ministries also provides a model for adoption by other countries in the Pacific.

With a mindset of gender-responsive budgeting, the Government of Fiji was able to address the immediate impacts of COVID-19.

Hashtags:

#GenderResponsiveBudgeting, #GenderEquality, #PFM, #GenderMainstreaming, #Fiji, #SDG5

Find out more:

- https://bit.ly/3BK3j58

Helping Tonga Strengthen its Public Sector Economy

Project Name: Building Macroeconomic Resilience Program

Region/Country: Pacific/Tonga

Sector and Themes: Governance and Public Sector Management

Year: 2019

Project Leader: Ananya Basu

The program has been critical for better management of government spending and costs.
—Lia Maka, chief executive officer, Tonga Public Services Commission

The grant will help Tonga strengthen its fiscal position by adopting prudent policies and better public financial management, and improve the country's business climate with policy, regulatory, and public enterprise reforms.

Development challenge

Like other small island developing states, Tonga is far from the mainstream of regional and global economic activity. Resources and current sources of income are limited, and the private sector is sparse. Governance and institutional issues, such as complex laws that have discouraged potential foreign investors, and public spending that has often outstripped public revenues, have not made economic growth and development any easier. Tonga, which buys more from the rest of the world than it sells, is exposed and vulnerable to external economic shocks.

Solution

ADB and Tonga employed policy-based support to work together on the country's root governance and institutional challenges under the Building Macroeconomic Resilience Program, with funding from the Asian Development Fund. The program provided $10.25 million as grants and approximately $4.15 million in concessional loans through 3 subprograms in 2016–2019. It was targeted at improving Tonga's fiscal position by adopting prudent policies and better public financial management and supporting the business climate by continuing policy, regulatory, and public enterprise reforms.

Knowledge products and services delivered

The TA support from ADB helped strengthen public financial management to boost tax revenue. It aided adjustment of the public service salary structure, and supported policy reforms to make the tax regime more productive and efficient. It raised the performance of the country's public enterprises and made the investment environment more hospitable to private businesses. The program also reviewed the public service salary and performance structures, and analyzed the private sector development environment in Tonga.

Impact and results

The program helped raise tax revenues as a share of GDP from 17.4% in the 2011 to 2015 fiscal years, to 21.0% in the 2017 to 2019 fiscal years. It introduced policy and legislative frameworks for foreign investment, contracting, and bankruptcy; and reformed five public enterprises to promote efficiency of service delivery. The project has helped government agencies improve management of public spending, and civil service performance has also improved. The second phase of the project strengthened public financial management to boost tax revenue, adjusted the public service salary structure, raised the performance of the country's public enterprises, and made the investment environment more hospitable to private businesses.

Lessons for replication

Lessons from the program include the importance of building ownership of reform through participation and consensus, incorporating the need for capacity and institutional development, and keeping the program design simple and flexible. Provision of significant TA to undertake knowledge work helps to underpin reforms.

Hashtags:
#Tonga, #Economy, #PublicSector, #Macroeconomics, #EconomicAffairs

Find out more:
- https://bit.ly/3AKMFRo

Building a Community of Integrity Champions in ADB

Project Name:	Are You an Integrity Champion? or iPLAY iACT: Making Learning Fun
Region/Country:	Philippines (Headquarters)
Sector and Themes:	Governance and Public Sector Management
Year:	2019
Project Leaders:	Knowledge and Communications Team, Office of Anticorruption and Integrity

" *I am grateful for your contribution and thoroughness in designing such an effective way of learning... the knowledge I grasped in such a short time is really wonderful.* "

—Sunila Ghimire, project analyst, ADB

ADB Managing Director General Woochung Um trying out the e-learning course on integrity.

Development challenge

Given the complexity and scale of anticorruption work, the demand for learning opportunities continues to grow year by year. The Knowledge and Communications Team of the Office of Anticorruption and Integrity focuses on strengthening the anticorruption skills of ADB staff and the public through knowledge products and learning events. As staff continue to work at ADB, there is a need to refresh themselves with the fundamental principles of anticorruption and integrity and apply the principles in real-world scenarios that will require their knowledge and critical thinking skills.

Solution

In 2019, the Office of Anticorruption and Integrity created Are You an Integrity Champion?, an e-learning course on anticorruption and integrity for all ADB staff. It provides multiple-choice questions and likely scenarios where the learner applies critical thinking and knowledge of ADB's Anticorruption Policy, Integrity Principles and Guidelines, Code of Conduct, and relevant administrative orders. The course uses gaming tools to motivate learners and facilitate learning.

Knowledge products and services delivered

Are You an Integrity Champion? is a refresher online course launched in 2019 to provide the learner with a review of concepts and guidelines introduced in the 2017 Anticorruption and Respect at Work (ARW) learning module. Learners enroll in a self-study mode and are expected to complete the course within 6 months of enrollment. The course has four levels, and learners must answer questions correctly to earn points indicated on a specific tile. Bonus points are awarded for giving the correct and speedy response, while penalty point deductions are given for incorrect answers. A puzzle must be completed at the end of each level and earns points. As the game remembers your highest score per level, it allows learners to replay the level that will change the sum of the scores. A ranking of top scorers is displayed on the initial interface of the module, and a digital certificate is awarded for each level completed.

Impact and results

When the ARW course was launched in 2017, 557 learners completed it. When Are You an Integrity Champion? was launched 2 years later, 759 learners played it 4,600 times.

The proportion of learning participants completing the ARW course went from 14% (557 out of a total of 3,971 learners) in 2017, to 20% (1,290 out of 6,619 learners) after ADB switched to online learning mode. This confirms that online learning is gaining ground as more people spend more time on electronic devices and prefer interactivity as a means of upgrading their skills. Under Strategy 2030, the course aims to reach more staff and stakeholders in ADB's DMCs, and increase awareness of integrity issues.

Lessons for replication

Online courses allow learners the ease of self-paced learning and training in required areas.

In 2019, the Office of Anticorruption and Integrity created Are You an Integrity Champion?, an e-learning course on anticorruption and integrity for all ADB staff.

Integrity booth at ADB.

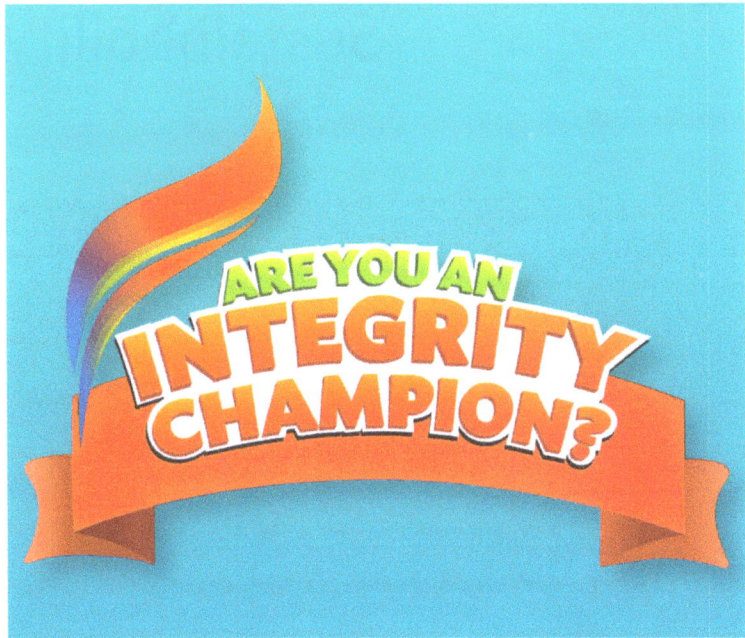

"

The two games have enabled us to see how many people are keen to play and learn. They also use the most basic and effective teaching method of repetition, which improves knowledge and awareness. They also assess the scores to establish that most players have a reasonable level of understanding of integrity and corruption."

—David Binns, director, Investigations Division, Office of Anticorruption and Integrity, ADB

Hashtags:
#AntiCorruption, #Integrity, #OAI, #eLearning, #CapacityBuilding, #Strategy2030, #Governance

Find out more:
- https://bit.ly/2Xc1q1Y

ADB Framework for Debt Sustainability Analysis

Project Name:	ADB Framework for Debt Sustainability Analysis
Region/Country:	Global
Sector and Themes:	Governance and Public Sector Management
Year:	2020–Present
Project Leaders:	Kaukab Naqvi and Benno Ferrarini

" *With timely support from Economic Research and Regional Cooperation Department, we were able to process the COVID-19 pandemic response operations in time to meet our clients' needs for financing.*

—Rommel Flores Rabanal, public sector economist, Pacific Department, ADB "

ADB needed a new framework to conduct debt sustainability analysis reflecting the COVID-19 environment.

Development challenge

The resulting lockdowns and containment measures from the COVID-19 pandemic have had economic and social costs. Panic over the crisis has led to financial market meltdowns. Financial institutions are facing a marked rise in nonperforming loans from a combination of declines in consumption, investment, tourism, and exports. Many of ADB's DMCs have seen a substantial decline in foreign direct investment and free falls in remittances. Tax systems seem to be collapsing; and with prolonged economic contractions, limited and deteriorating economic buffers, and heavy debt burdens, DMCs have little room to provide a proper response.

With weak financial and capital markets, most governments, unlike developed countries, are not able to introduce huge fiscal and monetary stimulus packages, consequently increasing their reliance on external borrowing.

Solution

ADB provided loans through its countercyclical support facility. This lending modality requires that the additional lending from ADB and from other development partners not jeopardize the debt sustainability of the borrowing countries. This required ADB's regional departments to conduct debt sustainability analysis to process the loans.

Before the pandemic, regional departments used to rely on debt sustainability analysis from the International Monetary Fund (IMF). However, with the severe disruption of the pandemic on the DMCs, the IMF's analysis, based on the prospects of economic growth and fiscal situation, became obsolete. ADB needed a new framework to conduct debt sustainability analysis reflecting the COVID-19 environment.

A team of economists from ADB's ERCD prepared a debt dynamic tool to analyze debt sustainability. In recognition of the uncertainty facing both ADB and its DMCs, ERCD adopted a more flexible scenario-based approach that has minimal data requirements, but still produces valuable insight about the likely debt trajectory in the medium term.

Knowledge products and services delivered

The debt dynamic tool framework enables ADB to carry out debt sustainability analysis using a methodology that is vetted by the IMF to ensure rigor and alignment with previous analyses. The new framework produces projections of debt-to-GDP ratios under different scenarios. It can estimate the baseline scenario that presumes no external lending, an alternate scenario based on lending from ADB and other development partners, and a total loan scenario that captures external lending from all the sources.

Impact and result

The flexibility with which the framework can be used enables ERCD to meet the demands of the regional

Azerbaijan's Public Debt Dynamics under Macroeconomic Scenarios
(Public debt-GDP ratio)

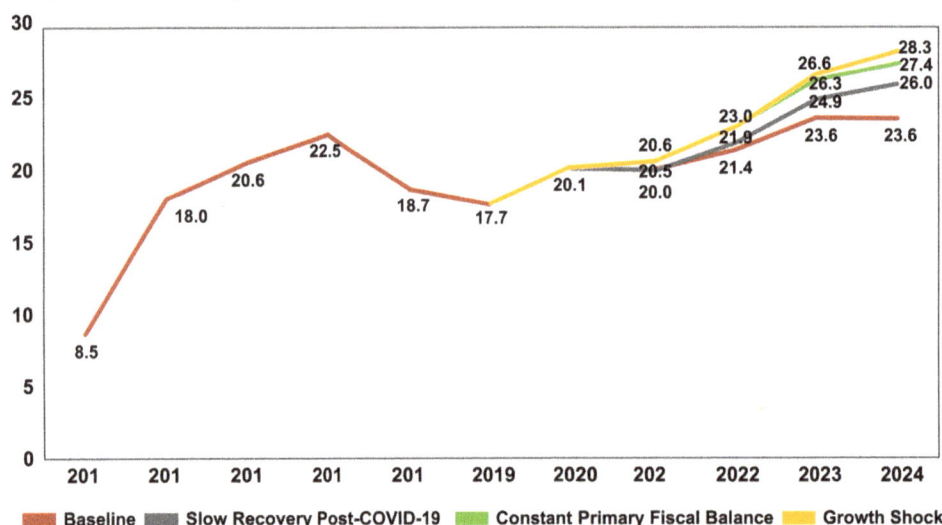

Public Debt (% of GDP)	2014	2015	2016	2017	2018	2019	2020	2021	2022	2023	2024
Baseline[a]	8.5	18.0	20.6	22.5	18.7	17.7	20.1	20.0	21.4	23.6	23.6
Slow recovery post-COVID-19[b]						17.7	20.1	20.0	21.9	24.9	26.0
Constant primary fiscal balance[c]						17.7	20.1	20.5	23.0	26.3	27.4
Growth shock[d]						17.7	20.1	20.6	23.0	26.6	28.3

COVID-19 = coronavirus disease, GDP = gross domestic products.
[a] Baseline scenario is based on ADB's projections without COVID-19 lending.
[b] The slow recovery post-COVID-19 scenario assumes that growth is half the baseline scenario's projections from 2022 onwards.
[c] The constant primary fiscal balance assumes that the primary fiscal balance remains unchanged throughout the projection period, equal to 2020.
[d] The growth shock scenario assumes growth that is 1 percentage point lower than in the baseline scenario.
Source: Asian Development Bank. 2021. *Azerbaijan-Debt Sustainability Analysis (internal document)*. Manila.

departments and help process the much-needed financing to DMCs well on time. As a result, while initially ADB announced a $6.5 billion package to address the immediate needs of the DMCs, by early September 2020, it enabled ADB to provide an additional $13 billion. ADB's timely response and assistance has helped its DMCs to mitigate the impact of crisis and plan for the post-COVID future.

Lessons for replication

The success of the project highlights the importance of teamwork and active cross-border engagement and collaboration. Agility was imperative for the framework to work; the "One ADB" approach was vital to help ensure timely processing of the loan documents.

> *ERCD has closely worked with Southeast Asia Department as a One ADB Team during the preparation of the Philippines: Second Health System Enhancement to Address and Limit COVID-19 with Asia Pacific Vaccine Access Facility (HEAL2). ERCD provided timely support to prepare the debt sustainability analysis as part of the documents for the project report.*
>
> **—Sakiko Tanaka, principal social sector specialist, Southeast Asia Department, ADB**

> *The timely inputs and the debt sustainability analysis prepared by ERCD has helped us to process $500 million in COVID-19 pandemic response loans for Uzbekistan, $100 million in loans for Azerbaijan, and $100 million in grants for Afghanistan.*
>
> **—Cigdem Akin, senior public management economist, Central and West Asia Department, ADB**

Hashtags:
#CovidResponse, #DebtSustainabilityAnalysis, #DebtSustainability, #PostCovidFuture, #ERCD #OneADB

Find out more:
- https://www.youtube.com/watch?v=eK6h8UXp9JY

Ensuring Consistent, Robust, and Timely Project Data for ADB

Project Name:	Financial Management Information Dashboard
Region/Country:	Southeast Asia/Philippines
Sector and Themes:	Governance and Public Sector Management
Year:	2019
Project Leader:	Sevil Maharramova

" I am very impressed. You just saved us money, time, and effort.

—Jesper Petersen, advisor and head, Portfolio, Results, Safeguards, and Gender Unit, Central and West Asia Department, ADB

ADB staff exploring the new Financial Management Information Dashboard.

Development challenge

A 2018 review of ADB's financial management found that available financial management data was limited and inconsistent, making it difficult to perform robust analysis. There was a lack of effective tools to monitor and report on projects and portfolio financial management performance. The various manual tools that existed within ADB operations departments used inconsistent assumptions and data definitions. These issues adversely impacted management decisions on how to improve ADB project processing and implementation and strengthen systems and institutions in its DMCs.

Solution

A team from ADB's Procurement, Portfolio, and Financial Management Department (PPFD) and the IT Department developed the Financial Management Information Dashboard (FMiD), a real-time monitoring and reporting solution on financial management compliance and performance for ADB management and staff. FMiD modernized business processes for providing relevant data and analytics. It also provided timely and relevant analytics to support the strengthening of governance and institutional capacity of DMCs.

Knowledge products and services delivered

FMiD provides relevant and consistent real-time data on a project's financial management performance, as well as analytics on DMCs' public financial management systems. The tool is accessible to all staff and ensures that there is "one source of truth" when analyzing and reporting financial management data. FMiD was introduced to users through technical briefings and workshops, and via an online tutorial explaining key functionalities and reports available through it.

Impact and results

FMiD was successfully launched in the first quarter of 2020. As of 31 December 2020, FMiD ranked fourth by number of users among existing ADB dashboards, with 178 users and 1,901 total views during its first year of operation. FMiD was used for presentation performance ratings and compliance for the second and fourth quarters of 2020 Operations Review Meeting reports, and for the monitoring of the ADB Corporate Results Framework indicator in the Development Effectiveness Review.

Lessons for replication

System enhancements introduced made financial management data readily available from eOps, the integrated system that manages ADB's project-related information and documents. Thus, financial management monitoring and reporting of compliance with loan covenants and agreements can easily be performed. FMiD is designed as a dynamic reporting tool, and PPFD will continue to incorporate more reports and analytics depending on the needs of ADB's operations departments and data available in eOps. The project also highlights the importance and strength of interdepartmental collaboration and the "One ADB" approach, building on seamless and effective cooperation between PPFD and IT department teams.

ADB Director General for Information Technology Department Shirin Hamid explained how the Financial Management Information Dashboard provides "live" data on the financial management performance of a project.

> *We appreciate that FMiD was developed in close collaboration with those who are dealing with data in the Information Technology Department and they have ensured the consistency of the definition and data sources with the ADB Data Dictionary.*
>
> **—Ayumi Konishi, former special senior advisor to the President, Office of the President, ADB**

> *Thank you for setting up the financial management portfolio analysis tool. It is helpful to monitor the status promptly and manage the projects efficiently.*
>
> **—Sorin Chung, financial management specialist, Southeast Asia Department, Urban Development and Water Division, ADB**

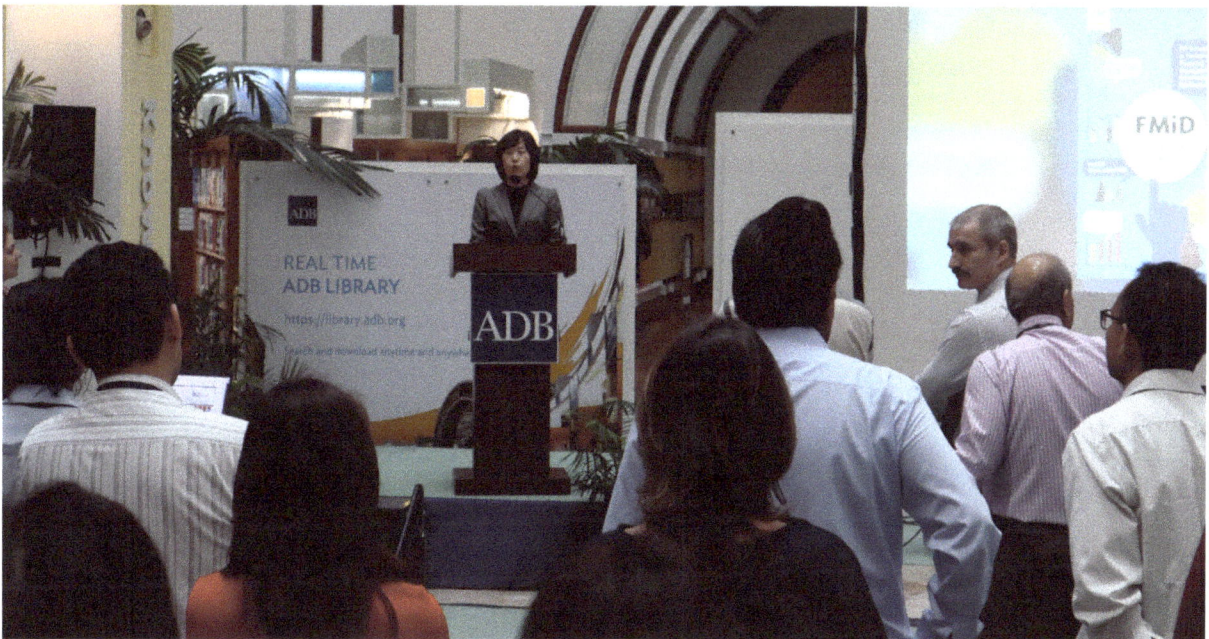

ADB Director General for Procurement, Portfolio, and Financial Management Department Risa Teng launched the Financial Management Information Dashboard in February 2020.

Hashtags:

#FinancialManagement, #BusinessProcess, #Innovation, #Digitalization, #Reporting, #Analytics #Strategy2030, #Monitoring, #Performance, #DataAnalysis

Restoring Connectivity and Flood Resiliency of Roads in Solomon Islands

Project Name: Transport Sector Flood Recovery Project

Region/Country: Pacific/Solomon Islands

Sector and Themes: Transport

Year: 2015–2019

Project Leader: Elma Morsheda

> *Communities in the east and west can still get to town now even when some main rivers are flooded... That means sick people can reach clinics and hospitals in town for treatment during heavy storms.*
>
> **—Mike Qaqara, Ministry of Infrastructure Development**

Daniel Manengelea, principal of Ruavatu Provincial Secondary School in East Guadalcanal and students attending the short-term project-specific graduate recruitment program.

Development challenge

In 2014, tropical cyclone Ita brought severe flooding to Honiara, the capital of Solomon Islands, and surrounding areas. The storm damaged and destroyed major infrastructure, and the Government of Solomon Islands declared a state disaster for Honiara and all of Guadalcanal province. Total losses were more than $107 million, the equivalent of 9.2% of Solomon Islands' GDP in 2014. The housing sector accounted for about 56%, and transport, 23%, of the total. A rapid assessment by ADB and other development partners determined that roads and bridges should be repaired immediately to minimize secondary impacts on the economy, and to restore connectivity to essential services. The government developed a recovery plan, which required almost $35 million in total reconstruction costs for the transport sector.

Solution

ADB approved the Transport Sector Flood Recovery Project to support the government's recovery plan. The project was aimed at restoring socioeconomic activities to at least pre-flood levels and bringing more resilient connectivity. The country's National Transport Plan 2011–2030 and the National Transport Fund, established with ADB TA, enabled the government to formally set out a policy framework in developing and maintaining transport infrastructure as well as improving the capacity of government agencies and the private sector toward sustainable transport management.

Knowledge products and services delivered

A design supervision consultant helped the Ministry of Infrastructure Development to conduct a feasibility study and design the civil works contract. The consultant also conducted baseline and post-project household surveys of the communities living in the areas surrounding the subproject sites. The civil works contract had 12 subprojects comprising construction and rehabilitation of infrastructure, which reestablished the connectivity between east and west of Guadalcanal province through Honiara. To help overcome an initial staff shortage in the ministry, a short-term project-specific graduate recruitment program enabled it to hire eight engineers from the University of the South Pacific, Solomon Islands, to contribute to the improvement of construction supervision.

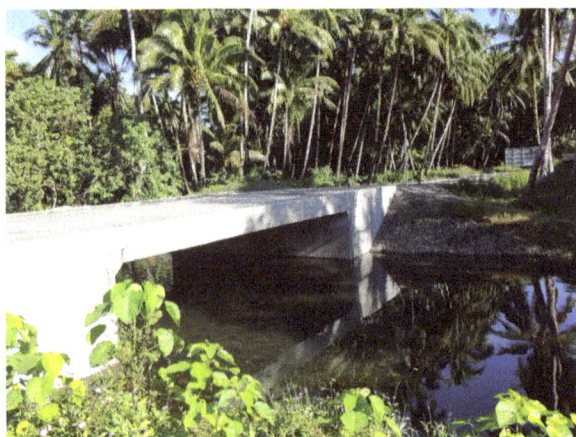

Impact and results

The post-project household survey found that beneficiaries were satisfied with the reconnected road, but the benefits from the reconnection depend on whether these are maintained. The survey provides input in improved services to ensure that connectivity remains sustainable over the anticipated 25-year life of the project. The government, through the Sustainable Transport Infrastructure Improvement Program, developed a transport infrastructure maintenance mechanism using the National Transport Fund, and is expanding its transport sector development to include physical, financial, and institutional aspects in enhancing the road services and asset management. The assignment of graduate engineers provided learning opportunities and enabled them to become part of a professional talent pool with practical experience.

More than simply restoring basic links to the usual standards, the project took a build-back-better approach.

> "
> We've marked the new bridges to track current water levels... If the river rises above a certain point, our evacuation plan goes into motion.
>
> **—Regina Pokana, sustainability and quality manager, Palm Oil Company, East Guadalcanal**

Lessons for replication

The sector approach used in constructing and rehabilitating linked roads and maintenance could be applied in future interventions. For Solomon Islands, employing graduate engineers will help them land jobs later. Similar projects should also include a thorough assessment of the country's weather, the government's capacity constraints, and the time required to assess the severity of damage and complete the feasibility study. They should also resolve land disputes over construction sites.

The project will help fund construction of vital infrastructure designed to be more resilient against disasters and other climate threats.

> *People previously had no choice but to carry their heavy market-bound loads through the river in wheelbarrows to get to a truck on the other side. If you missed the truck to town, that was it. Now, with the better roads and bridges, there are several market trips a day.*
>
> **—Daniel Manengelea, principal, Ruavatu Provincial Secondary School, East Guadalcanal**

Hashtags:

#Connectivity, #Flood, #Recovery, #SolomonIslands, #Transport, #DisasterResilience, #Sustainability

Find out more:

- https://bit.ly/3DK2BFs

New Roads and Improved Infrastructure for Afghanistan

Project Name:	Qaisar–Dari Bum Road Project
Region/Country:	Central and West Asia/Afghanistan
Sector and Themes:	Transport
Year:	2017
Project Leaders:	Ganesh Kailasam and Witoon Tawisook

> *The road works should be good for our small community.*
> *I may even set up a small family business, start a dairy farm,*
> *or raise chickens.*
>
> **—Mahane, resident, Tagab Ismael**

The project will help promote economic and social development and reduce poverty by rehabilitating the primary road network damaged during 2 decades of conflict and neglect.

Development challenge

Rugged terrain, a sparse network of poorly maintained roads, harsh winters, and the impact of armed conflict have left Afghanistan's thinly spread population and widely dispersed communities isolated from each other. Underdeveloped, worn-out, and barely passable roads have kept the sick from hospitals, children from schools, and crops from markets. The demanding geography, security issues, and associated high costs have long frustrated efforts to fully develop Afghanistan's roads.

Solution

This project in the northwest region, financed by a $330 million ADF grant approved in 2017, will provide the last missing link to complete the rehabilitation of Afghanistan's major circular highway, the 90-kilometer Ring Road. It will also fund the installation of road tolling facilities including toll plazas, computers, and communications equipment, and weighing machines for the road. The project includes drainage and modern highway safety features, as well as roadside infrastructure facilities, including rural access roads, and a community development program for 60 local communities. The road will be designed and constructed to incorporate disaster risk and climate change adaptation features, which are critical for the country to increase the resiliency of its infrastructure. The long-awaited improvements will make overland travel and trade between Afghanistan and neighboring Iran, Pakistan, Tajikistan, Turkmenistan, and Uzbekistan easier and more efficient.

The project will integrate lessons learned in provisioning infrastructure in a fragile environment.

Knowledge products and services delivered

Besides rehabilitation of the Qaisar–Bala Murghab section of the Herat–Andkhoy road, the project also provides for knowledge services including construction supervision and monitoring support, and incremental project management such as engagement of external auditors to audit project accounts. It also includes HIV prevention and anti-human trafficking awareness activities.

Impact and results

Road improvements are expected to provide better access to markets, schools, and health services, and more job opportunities in the roadside communities. Vehicle operating costs on the project roads are projected to drop by 30%. By 2023, with the provision of the Ring Road's missing link, the number of provincial capitals and major towns connected to the regional highway network is set to increase by 15% from 2017. The project has the support of local communities, which can enjoy direct and immediate benefits. Overall, the project and the Ring Road improvements will integrate the country's northwest with the rest of Afghanistan. That will stimulate economic growth and further infrastructure development. The Ring Road improvement is expected to open Afghanistan not only to its closest neighbors but, through them, to the wider world and opportunities beyond.

The road incorporates disaster risk and climate change adaptation features.

Lessons for replication

Installation of road tolling facilities including toll plazas, computers, and communications equipment, as well as weighing machines for roads should be done in an efficient manner. The roads should be designed and constructed to incorporate disaster risk and climate change adaptation features, especially in disaster-prone areas.

> *The Ring Road Project has impacted the community as a whole. Completion of the project will influence positive change mainly on the environment, economy, and social life of the communities.*
> **—Project manager, Ministry of Public Works**

> *This project and the Ring Road improvements overall will integrate the country's northwest with the rest of Afghanistan. That will stimulate economic growth and further infrastructure development.*
>
> **—Manager, Qaisar–Laman project component**

Improvement of disaster risk reduction and climate change adaptation capacity in the road subsector is under preparation.

Hashtags:
#Afghanistan, #Transport, #Roads, #Infrastructure, #EconomicGrowth

Find out more:
- https://bit.ly/3DK2BFs
- https://bit.ly/3lGgLBf

Community Empowerment Boosts Sanitation and Water Supply Services in Nepal

Project Name:	Second Small Towns Water Supply and Sanitation Sector Project
Country:	Nepal
Sector and Themes:	Urban Development
Year:	2009
Project Leader:	Shiva Prasad Paudel

> *With 24-hour tap water supply in my own house, I do not spend so much time fetching water. With the saved time, now I am raising pigs and some poultry to sell.*
> **—Ranjana Jogi, beneficiary, Indrapur Water Supply Subproject, Morang District**

ADB is helping Nepal improve access to water and sanitation services in small towns throughout the country.

Development challenge

Nepal's small urban centers have only rudimentary water and sanitation systems, and pressure on them has increased as more economic migrants have arrived from the hill regions and countryside. Water availability is intermittent in many urban areas, with half of the gravity flow systems in the hills in need of major repair, and more than half of the tube wells in the lowland Terai region being contaminated.

Solution

The Second Small Towns Water Supply and Sanitation Sector Project, financed with $45 million from the ADF, upgraded water services for about 20 towns. Communities shared the service delivery cost equally with the government. By training

community members in operational management of the small water supply schemes and placing major responsibilities for governance in the hands of local people, the project sought to reinforce a sense of ownership and a stake in the operation and maintenance of water facilities infrastructure.

Knowledge products and services delivered

Water user and sanitation committees were trained in operations and maintenance and financial management. They then decided on the technologies to be used in the community's systems. Community members also decided how much upfront cash they would need to operate a new water system and how much to draw from their

Town Development Fund, a financial intermediary which on-lent a portion of ADB grant to water users' associations for the construction of water supply systems. The project design monitoring framework and gender equality and social inclusion action plan ensured that women and targeted vulnerable communities benefited from all project outputs. The capacity development trainings targeted women, who take a major role in household water management and care works, and women were involved in every aspect of the project.

Impact and results

By 2017, 21 town projects were completed and after 1 year all the systems have since been operated and maintained by the users. More than 370,000 people have access to improved water supply systems, and more than 278,000 people have access to improved sanitation facilities. The water supply and sanitation facilities reduced women's time poverty, enhanced the economic empowerment, and helped improve gender equality in human development, decision making, and leadership. Women's engagement in capacity building enabled them to make their voices heard and be part of the decision-making processes. The Town Development Fund continues to support all the water users and sanitation committees for efficient operation of the system by providing necessary training, preparing tariff guidelines, developing business plans, and carrying out other capacity building activities. An effort to improve the urban water supply sector is also in progress.

Lessons for replication

The project showcased the importance of capacity building initiatives, and particularly of women playing an important role in design, financing, and operation and maintenance. The project offers lessons for similar projects to involve local communities right from the inception of the project, and for them to own and govern the water services, thus ensuring its sustainability.

The project also improved governance and capacity for project management and operation.

> " *I am blind by birth and my husband died many years ago. I live in my parents' house. My life was totally dependent on others, even for getting water to drink and for other uses. My life completely changed when this project selected me as one of the recipients for free tap connection and toilet under the project's output-based aid. This has decreased my dependency on others, building my self-confidence and ability.*
>
> **—Damanta Adhikari, Lamahi Project Component**

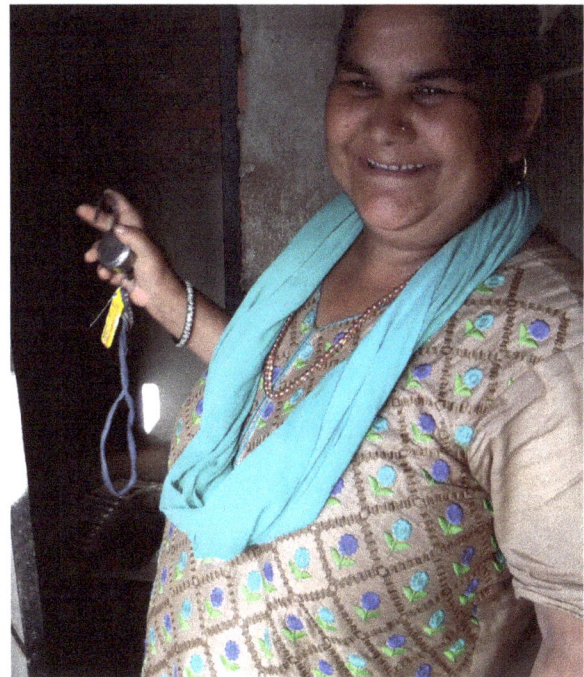

The project ensured that women and targeted vulnerable communities benefited from all project outputs.

Hashtags:
#Nepal, #WaterSanitation, #UrbanWaterSupply, #Sanitation

Find out more:
- https://bit.ly/3AGUlo0
- https://bit.ly/3DK2BFs

Building a Climate-Resilient "Sponge City" in Jiangxi Province, People's Republic of China

Project Name: Jiangxi Pingxiang Integrated Rural–Urban Infrastructure Development

Region/Country: East Asia/People's Republic of China

Sector and Themes: Urban Development

Year: 2015–2022

Project Leader: Stefan Rau

Picture a whole city that absorbs, harvests, stores, filters, purifies, and slowly releases rainwater, like a sponge.

ADB is working with the People's Republic of China to address flooding and other water management problems in Jiangxi Province, which are holding back development and growth.

Development challenge

Situated in flood-prone Jiangxi province, Pingxiang—one of the poorer cities in the PRC—is hindered by inadequate flood risk management, suboptimal wastewater and solid waste management, and environmental pollution. Within the city boundaries, there is a clear rural–urban divide. If unsustainable urban development were to persist, the social, economic, and environmental divide between urban and rural areas of Pingxiang would worsen. Pingxiang was chosen as one of 12 cities for industry transformation and diversification, and for implementing an innovative approach to rural–urban integration.

Solution

ADB collaborated with the Jiangxi provincial and Pingxiang municipal governments on sustainable urban–rural development with a $150 million loan. The project contributed to making Pingxiang a pilot "Sponge City"—a flood-resilient urban and rural territory and community. It designed and implemented best practices in integrated ecological flood risk management and river rehabilitation using a green infrastructure and nature-based solutions approach. It also integrated farmland irrigation. The project supported wastewater collection and treatment in county cities and towns by expanding sewer pipe networks and building state-of-the-art wastewater treatment plants. The project improved connectivity between the city, small towns, and industrial areas with construction of a new 44-kilometer rural–urban road.

Knowledge products and services delivered

The project continues to implement several features and knowledge services. These include capacity building of PRC government officials through workshops and on-the-job training, study tours, and stakeholder technical consultation. Training materials on the Pingxiang project's approach and design have benefited many. The project was publicized through articles in Chinese newspapers and on the ADB website. A book *Creating Livable Cities in Asia*,[32] includes this project and a description of the sponge city concept.

Impact and results

The project is well on the way to helping Pingxiang establish itself as an important and innovative pilot "Sponge City" covering urban and rural areas. All river rehabilitation works are under construction, and some are already completed. This is expected to benefit about 308,000 farmers and rural and urban residents directly from reduced flood risk.

A total of 96 kilometers of sewer pipelines have been installed. A wastewater treatment plant and associated sewers are under construction, benefiting around 175,000 residents. Road construction and associated safety and public transport features as well as landscape improvements have been completed. The new road financed by the project will benefit about 247,000 residents and positively impact villages, schools, and industrial areas.

The project is financing flood protection works, river and wetlands rehabilitation, irrigation system upgrades, and wastewater treatment in four main urban sub-centers in the province, including Pingxiang.

---

[32]   ADB. 2021. *Creating Livable Asian Cities*. Manila.

"

We have been suffering from more and severe floods in recent years and the project will be reducing the risk of floods for many people in Lianhua county. We are very grateful for the integration of wetland rehabilitation and improving flood resilience which will create benefits for our residents, and also attract tourists as they will enjoy the wetlands and make Lianhua an even more pleasant as well as safer place to live and visit.

—He Tian Hua, vice mayor, Lianhua County

Lessons for replication

Cities can benefit from lessons learned from this project. The integrated approach of managing rivers on a catchment basis and applying ecosystem-based adaptation and nature-based solutions is cost effective, delivers a high-level of flood protection, and delivers additional ecosystem service benefits like water cleansing and filtration, urban air quality improvement, recreational amenities for residents, and land value increase.

Climate-resilient farming and rural–urban flood risk partnerships are among the innovative features that may be replicated elsewhere. Other municipalities can look at the strategic approaches to climate risk assessments and investments in rural or peri-urban subcenters to promote inclusive development. Finally, the project provides insights on engaging local communities on reducing environmental pollution and increasing road safety.

Using inteligently planned urban green spaces as blue-green networks will retain, naturally infiltrate, and slow down stone water. Asia's cities can significantly reduce the risk of floods and manage water resources in a sustainable way, while also making cities more livable and green.

Hashtags:
#PRC, #Jiangxi, #Pingxiang, #UrbanDevelopment, #SpongeCity, #Floods, #ClimateResilience

Devising a Flood Early Warning System in Kolkata

Project Name:	Flood Forecasting and Early Warning System for the City of Kolkata
Region/Country:	South Asia/India
Sector and Themes:	Urban Development
Year:	2017
Project Leader:	Ashwin Hosur Viswanath

" *Natural calamities, including heavy rain, can occur any time. This system will reduce economic loss and impacts on livelihood and improve flood awareness and safety at the community level.*

—Sovan Chatterjee, mayor, Kolkata City "

ADB has been supporting Kolkata to become a more livable city through integrated planning and phased investments for building resilience and improving urban services.

Development challenge

Kolkata has 4 million people exposed to flooding risks, with 1,800 milliliters of annual rainfall, of which 80% falls during the monsoon. The topography and tidal range (the height difference between high tide and low tide) exacerbate the situation, as does high population density.

Solution

ADB sponsored the Kolkata Environment Improvement Investment Program (KEIIP) that assisted the Kolkata Municipal Corporation (KMC) in making a smart and resilient city by modernizing financial, administrative, and asset management systems; reducing urban flood risks; improving land use planning; and developing their capacity to reach citizens through introduction of a flood forecasting and early warning system.

Being a people-centered flood-forecasting tool, the early warning system empowered individuals, communities, and other stakeholders to act quickly and appropriately to reduce flood risks. Predictive modeling, historical flood assessment from remote sensing, and consultation with citizens and borough engineers helped identify locations for real-time data collection on rainfall and flood risk, which were then verified during the monsoon.

Knowledge products and services delivered

The flood forecasting and early warning system was developed through an ADB TA program supported by the Urban Climate Change Resilience Trust Fund. A team from TARU Leading Edge Pvt. Ltd., PricewaterhouseCoopers, and Antea Group assisted KMC to design and implement the system. The Rockefeller Foundation and the governments of Switzerland and the United Kingdom were the project's financing partners.

This is the first comprehensive city-level early warning system in India. It provides real-time information from more than 300 Internet of Things-based multifunctional sensors to provide forecasts throughout the city, enabling informed decision making before and during disasters and help reduce loss and damage. It gives updates on multiple types of data and information including flooding, air quality, heat stress, and humidity, accessible via the K-Flood website and through the K-Flood app, which issues mobile phone alerts and has a monitoring system to inform city residents, among others.

Impact and results

The city was provided with a comprehensive forecasting system that gives real-time information on inundation, temperature, air quality, and other climate-related data that can help and improve the lives of various stakeholders.

KMC has also been simultaneously improving the city's urban services and climate resilience under KEIIP. It has been systematically expanding sewerage and drainage network in Kolkata, including peripheral flood-prone areas; increasing sewage

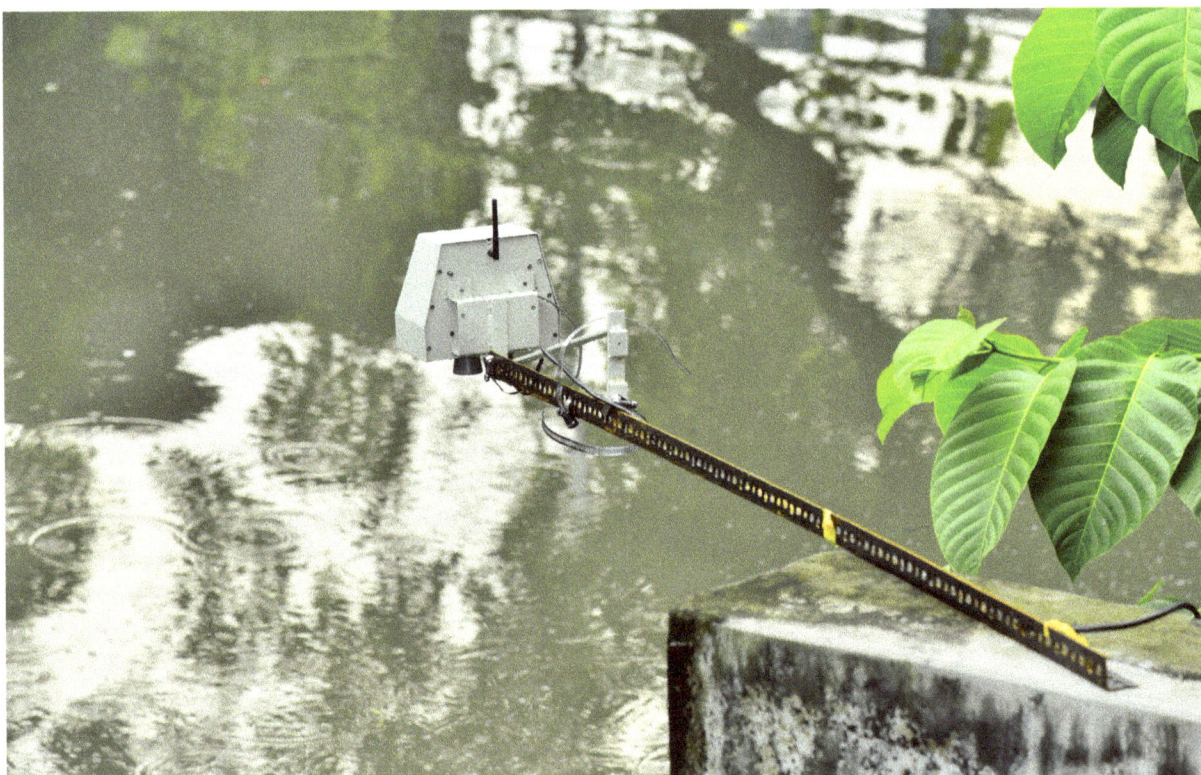

The system provides forecasts and real-time updates on rainfall and inundation levels, among other climate and environmental data, thereby strengthening the city's resilience.

> *The Kolkata drainage system is a very complex one, involving underground networks and hundreds of pumping stations, and it requires a lot of expertise and information to handle the storms and the big rains. Sometimes there are huge rains but the pumping stations are situated 3–4 kilometers away from that area. This system helps the pump operators plan better as the sensors alert them of any flow that goes over permissible limits.*
>
> **—Soumya Ganguly, KEIIP, Kolkata Municipal Corporation**

treatment capacity; improving water supply through reductions in nonrevenue water; managing solid waste; and increasing operational efficiencies and building capacity to better sustain the services it provides. Flooding has already been reduced in about 4,800 hectares, and KMC expects further flood reduction in more than 6,000 hectares covered under the projects.

Lessons for replication

Many of the existing pumping stations are old and are not amenable to control and automation. This necessitates capture of pumping data from basic sensors. The pumping stations have corrosive and dark environments, especially within the sumps, which reduces the life of sensors, so they need regular maintenance.

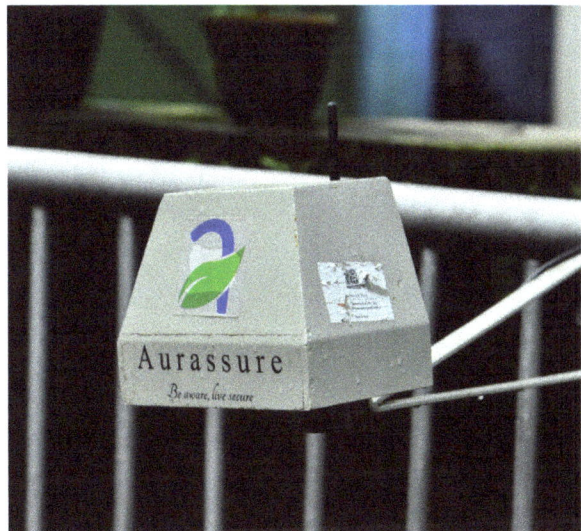

This is the first comprehensive city-level early warning system in India.

Hashtags:
#India, #Kolkata, #FloodForecasting, #Floods, #NaturalDisasters

Find out more:
- https://bit.ly/3p4HLwo
- https://bit.ly/3aJqtwo
- https://bit.ly/3mYuTFu

Protecting the Meghna River—A Sustainable Water Resource for Dhaka

Project Name:	Strengthening Monitoring and Enforcement in the Meghna River for Dhaka's Sustainable Water Supply
Country:	South Asia/Bangladesh
Sector and Themes:	Water
Year:	2014–2019
Project Leader:	Farhat Jahan Chowdhury

Pollution monitoring and mapping, engagement of local watchdog groups, and other measures implemented by the technical assistance will sustain this investment.

Expanding sustainable safe water supply in Dhaka City is a major activity of the sector to help the government achieve 100% access to water supply.

Development challenge

The Dhaka Water Supply and Sewerage Authority (DWASA) depends heavily on groundwater for supplying an area of approximately 400 square kilometers in Dhaka city. Current groundwater abstraction is beyond sustainable yields. The water quality in rivers surrounding Dhaka is rapidly deteriorating and quantity is inadequate. Bangladesh has identified Meghna River as a new source of water supply. However, DWASA does not have a legal mandate to regulate pollution in bodies of water. Rather, keeping the Meghna River clean and ensuring sustainable use falls under the mandate of the Department of Environment (DOE). By 2021,

Meghna River will account for more than 40% of DWASA's water supply. To avoid deterioration of water quality and ensure sustainable water supply, it is critical to strengthen the monitoring and enforcement mechanism for the river. However, the DOE is severely understaffed and lacks the institutional capacity to comprehensively act against violators.

Solution

With financing from the Japan Fund for Poverty Reduction, ADB worked closely with the DOE and DWASA to establish a robust monitoring and reporting system for the Meghna River. The project entailed analyzing existing policy and regulatory frameworks, demarcating different agencies' responsibilities, and establishing a reporting system whereby relevant stakeholders could report unlawful polluting activities. The project also piloted an incentive system to encourage pollution-control measures.

Knowledge products and services delivered

Monitoring and enforcement of the river was significantly improved by establishing eight watchdog groups, issuing monitoring reports, and strengthening six DOE labs. An ecologically critical area (ECA) on both sides of the Meghna River was identified, surveyed, and mapped. Polluting industries can no longer be established in this area. A pollution-control incentive system to encourage pollution-control measures was piloted. The project provided training programs, workshops, and seminars to build the capacity of stakeholders. There were also stakeholder consultations and public awareness campaigns on the environment, ECAs, and pollution along the river sections.

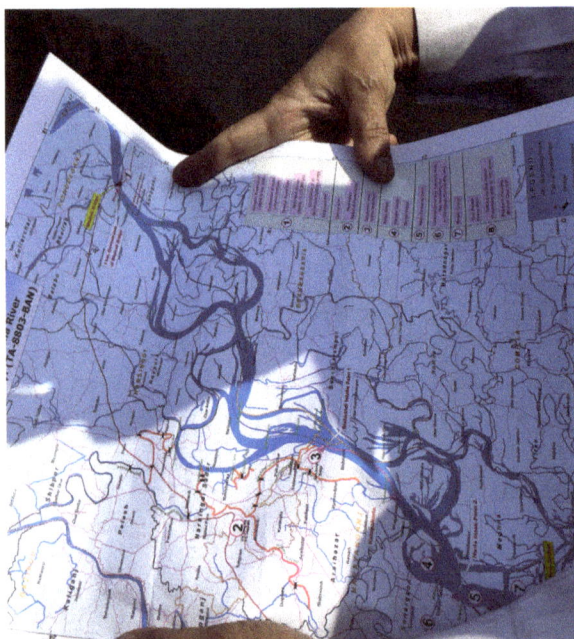

A national seminar to present key findings was held. ADB included another project in its pipeline for 2021 while the Agence Française de Développement and Dutch government-initiated projects continue their support for protection of the Meghna River. Protecting the Meghna River: A Sustainable Water Resource for Dhaka[33] was published, which assessed the water quality of the Meghna River and explored its potential as an alternative water source for Dhaka city.

Impact and results

The Meghna River Master Plan was initiated in August 2018. A Joint DOE–DWASA Institutional Setup was formulated to implement the results of the TA with the intention to support $1.3 billion investment in Dhaka's sustainable water supply. As the enforcement capacity of DOE was built through training, inspectors were able to impose fines on the polluting industries at the Meghna catchment area.

Watchdog groups issued monitoring reports and strengthened the DOE labs. The support also enabled the formulation of a scenario-based

The project focuses on strengthening monitoring and enforcement of Meghna River's quality for Dhaka's sustainable water supply.

---

[33] ADB. 2019. *Protecting the Meghna River: A Sustainable Water Resource for Dhaka.* Manila.

pollution model that will guide government on the requirement of pollution control. The project enabled improved knowledge on water quality, pollution sources, and economic and ecological resources of the Meghna River through studies and reports. Innovative cleaner production principles piloted in industrial clusters has reduced wastewater discharge, energy savings, and a 10%–30% reduction in chemical consumption.

Lessons for replication

Lessons could be drawn from the development of the geographical information system-linked pollution map, the market-based incentive system for pollution control, and the overall monitoring and reporting system. Understanding the stakeholder and data-driven process of designating parts of the river as ECAs could provide insights on how such a contentious policy objective could be achieved. The training programs, workshops, and seminars are a rich resource for future capacity building in the field. Active participation from a wide range of stakeholders contributed to the project's success.

The support also helped in the formulation of a scenario-based pollution model.

Hashtags:
#Bangladesh, #MeghnaRiver, #RiverProtection, #Monitoring, #Enforcement, #GISmap #SouthAsia

Find out more:
- https://bit.ly/2YUKsWQ
- https://bit.ly/2XhpuAI
- https://bit.ly/3DGok0Z
- https://bit.ly/3aFksRA

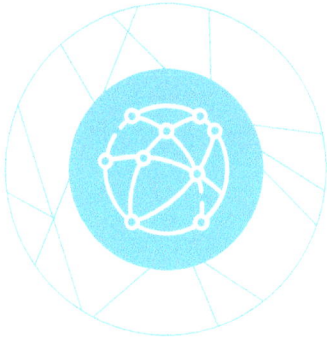

Climate Resilience Amid Economic Reform in Tonga

Project Name: Climate Resilience Sector Project

Region/Country: Pacific/Tonga

Sector and Themes: Multisector

Year: 2017

Project Leader: Ranishka Wimalasena

> *The relocation of Ha'apai's Niu'ui Hospital is a living, breathing example of the multiple benefits that may be gained from building public infrastructure back better.*
>
> **—Amelia Afuha'amango Tu'ipulotu, minister of health, Tonga**

The project will mainstream climate resilience into development planning and address country priorities focusing on the most vulnerable sectors and communities.

Development challenge

Tonga ranks second in the world for disaster risks. It is susceptible to cyclones, floods, and droughts. Increased ocean temperatures have caused coral bleaching and destruction of habitats for reef species. All these factors have caused significant economic losses to Tonga's economy, including destruction of infrastructure and habitat.

Solution

In partnership with Australia and the World Bank, ADB provided more than $30 million in budget support in 2009, 2013, and 2016 to Tonga to improve its climate resilience and undertake an ambitious economic reform program. This program was supported under the Climate Resilience Sector Project by a wide range of capacity building activities and the piloting of resilient infrastructure investments to be replicated elsewhere in the country.

Knowledge products and services delivered

Besides providing for infrastructure investments in renewable energy, climate resilience, and water and sanitation, ADB worked closely with government to improve its financial management capacity, spurring economic growth to create jobs and reduce poverty. It worked closely with the government to incorporate climate resilience within their planning and budgeting processes. It also comprised project finance through a Climate Change Trust Fund launched in 2013 that finances a range of low-cost and locally appropriate solutions for climate resilience, with suitable investments identified and implemented by civil society organizations and local communities.

More than 1,200 people from relevant public and private sectors have participated in climate change-related short courses. Twenty undergraduates completed university degrees and 19 government staff graduated with relevant certifications. The project also improved meteorological monitoring systems for better forecasting and early warning.

Impact and results

On 11 January 2014, Cyclone Ian, the most powerful storm ever recorded in Tonga's waters, passed directly over the Ha'apai group in the northeast of Tonga. Niu'ui Hospital was heavily damaged. The project helped to relocate the hospital to the highest point of the island and built back better with new features including a 500,000-liter rainwater storage tank. The hospital now also functions as a community evacuation center in times of disaster. Other benefits of the project included enhanced climate resilience for a some schools; construction of four evacuation roads in Eua and Tongatapu, Tonga's main island; enhanced coastal protection for 2 kilometers of continuous coastline; establishment of seven special management marine areas; and the

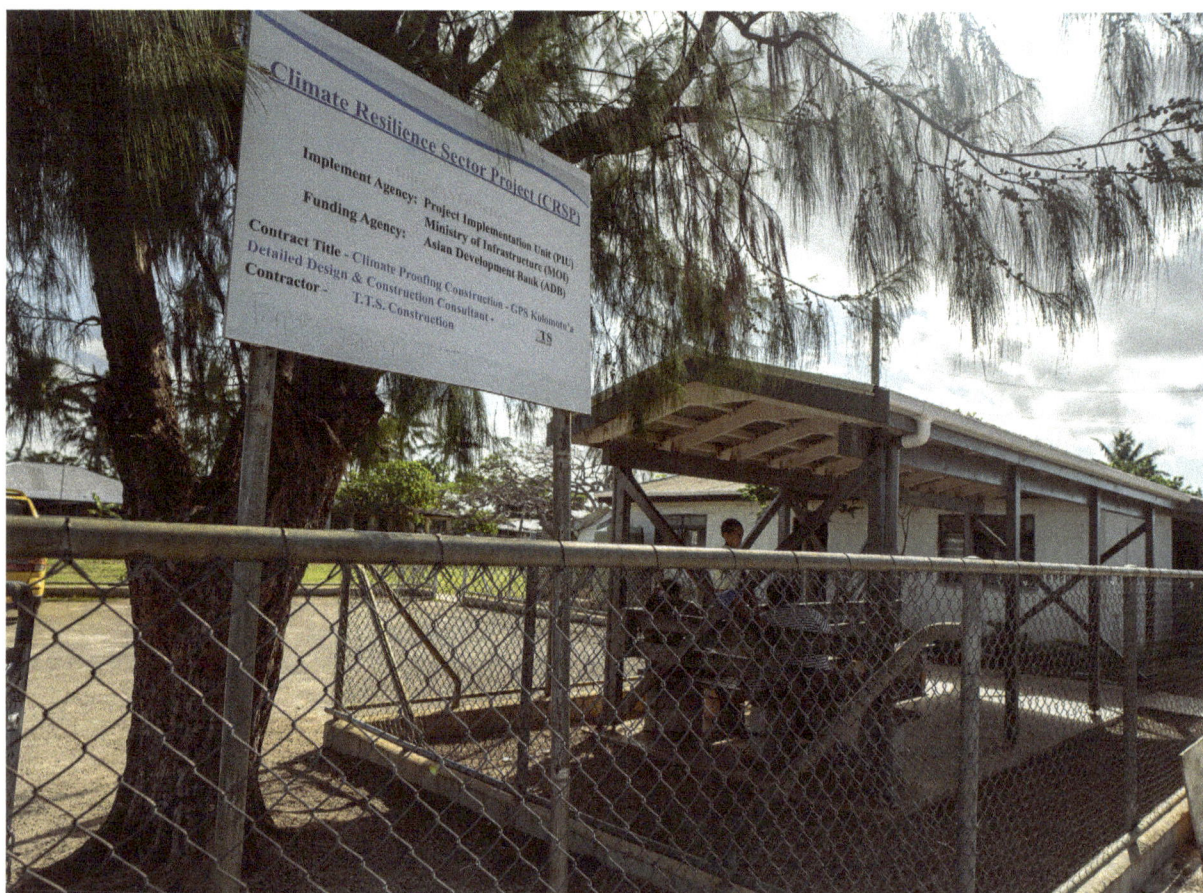

The project provided information, tools, and legislative frameworks needed to introduce climate change considerations into government and sector planning and budgeting processes.

introduction of a sustainable financing mechanism to ensure that vulnerable communities have access to climate-responsive community investments vital to livelihoods.

Lessons for replication

This project provides replicable solutions on aspects of improved performance, safety, and better public health outcomes through reliable services for public usage and for natural disasters. Mainstreaming resilience into corporate planning and day-to-day activities are critical in this context to ensure both financial and human resources accompany necessary policy reform. The project systematically built capacity in legislation, improved monitoring of climate data and information, increased ecosystem resilience in infrastructure investments and established a sustainable financing mechanism for community-based adaption investments.

The project helped provide access to resources to address the climate change risk priorities of the government, as well as those of vulnerable communities through a combination of "soft" and "hard" measures.

Hashtags:

#Tonga, #ClimateResilience, #Green, #Infrastructure

Find out more:

- https://bit.ly/3AGQIUw
- https://bit.ly/3vfHS9F

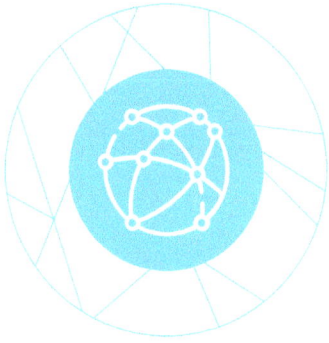

Demographic Change, Productivity, and the Role of Technology

Project Name:	Asian Economic Integration: Building Knowledge for Policy Dialogue, 2018–2021
Region/Country:	Regional/All Developing Member Countries
Sector and Themes:	Multisector
Year:	2018–Present
Project Leaders:	Cyn-Young Park and Aiko Kikkawa Takenaka

" *I found it wonderful to analyze the changes in the demographics of Asian countries... and to analyze the role that technology can play in combating the acceleration of aging and the declining working population.*

—Izumi Ohno, director, Japan International Cooperation Agency Research Institute "

Former ADB Chief Economist and Director General Yasuyuki Sawada presents the key findings of the AEIR 2019/2020 at the Research Institute of Economy, Trade and Industry (RIETI) in Tokyo, Japan, in November 2019.

Development challenge

Improving a country's educational profile can help ensure a constant stream of quality human capital. Countries need to acknowledge that while demographic transition is irreversible, economic impact can still be positive depending on the policy response. As such, it is crucial for economies in the Asia and Pacific region to explore policies that cater to the changing demographics and technologies that encourage the aging population to remain active for economic development.

Solution

ADB's ERCD worked closely with the Sustainable Development and Climate Change Department's technology, social development, education, and health thematic groups, and regional departments, to publish the Asian Economic Integration Report 2019/2020: Demographic Change, Productivity, and the Role of Technology (AEIR).[34] ERCD set up a joint event with the Social Development Thematic Group on employment and education for the elderly, and another event with the Education Thematic Group on digital skills and lifelong learning. ERCD also actively collaborated with many academic institutions and think tanks across the region.

---

[34]   ADB. 2019. *Asian Economic Integration Report 2019/2020: Demographic Change, Productivity, and the Role of Technology.* Manila.

Knowledge products and services delivered

AEIR made valuable recommendations on how aging populations can contribute to economic development, including how innovation and technology can turn demographic headwinds to tailwinds. It also made policy recommendations for ADB's 49 diverse DMCs to help them make the most of an aging workforce. It is a valuable resource for four types of countries looking to leverage technology to tackle population aging:

- fast aging and above median education,
- fast aging and below median education,
- slow aging and below median education, and
- slow aging and above median education.

The findings of the report were actively disseminated at policy and population aging events in Tokyo, Bangkok, and Hawaii, and via social media.

Impact and results

The publication proved to be a valuable resource for aging economies in Asia looking to leverage technology and innovative policies to effectively deal with the demographic transition. It provides concrete policy recommendations on the types of technology appropriate for each country, and highlights the reforms required in social security, labor markets, lifelong learning, and innovation to capture the gains from the demographic transition.

Public seminar on the Asian Economic Integration Report 2019/2020 held in Hawaii in November 2019. The panelists include economists in the field of demography, particularly aging. From left, ADB's Aiko Kikkawa Takenaka; ARC Centre of Excellence in Population Ageing Research Director John Piggott; University of California, Los Angeles Professor Kathleen McGarry; East-West Center and University of Hawaii at Manoa Senior Fellow and Professor Sang-Hyop Lee; and former ADB Chief Economist and Director General Yasuyuki Sawada.

Knowledge from the report has been used in various policy processes and programs including the G20's Think 20 initiative, and WHO's Regional Action Plan on Healthy Aging in the Western Pacific. It also formed the basis of Sri Lanka's national report on population aging. ADB's expertise at the intersection of population, aging, technology, and economic growth has attracted interest from Columbia University to collaborate on the Columbia World Project on Sustainable Aging; and the Government of Thailand for assistance in encouraging digital technology among the older adults in the country.

Lessons for replication

The AEIR and associated database are a valuable resource for a diversity of developing countries looking to leverage technology to tackle population aging. Other projects could also learn from the effective information dissemination and marketing strategies adopted for the AEIR.

The 2019/2020 report features a theme chapter on "Demographic Change, Productivity, and the Role of Technology," which explores the role and potential of technology in boosting the productivity of an aging economy.

Hashtags:
#DemographicChange, #Population, #Aging, #Technology, #EconomicIntegration #RegionalCooperation

Find out more:
- https://bit.ly/3lHLs9t
- https://bit.ly/3ACX2H6

The Road Ahead

Knowledge can only be power when it is shared where it is needed. Looking ahead, with a sound Knowledge Management Action Plan supporting ADB's Strategy 2030, the bank is well positioned to produce tailored knowledge solutions as part of its advisory role to DMCs. That plan lays out the right steps to ensure that all of ADB's knowledge is captured in a retrievable form, and easily available to all who can benefit from it. As part of that ongoing process, this book will be the first edition of an annual online publication that will showcase ADB's latest knowledge solutions.

To learn even more about ADB's knowledge solutions, check out ADB's TEDx-style talks and podcasts.

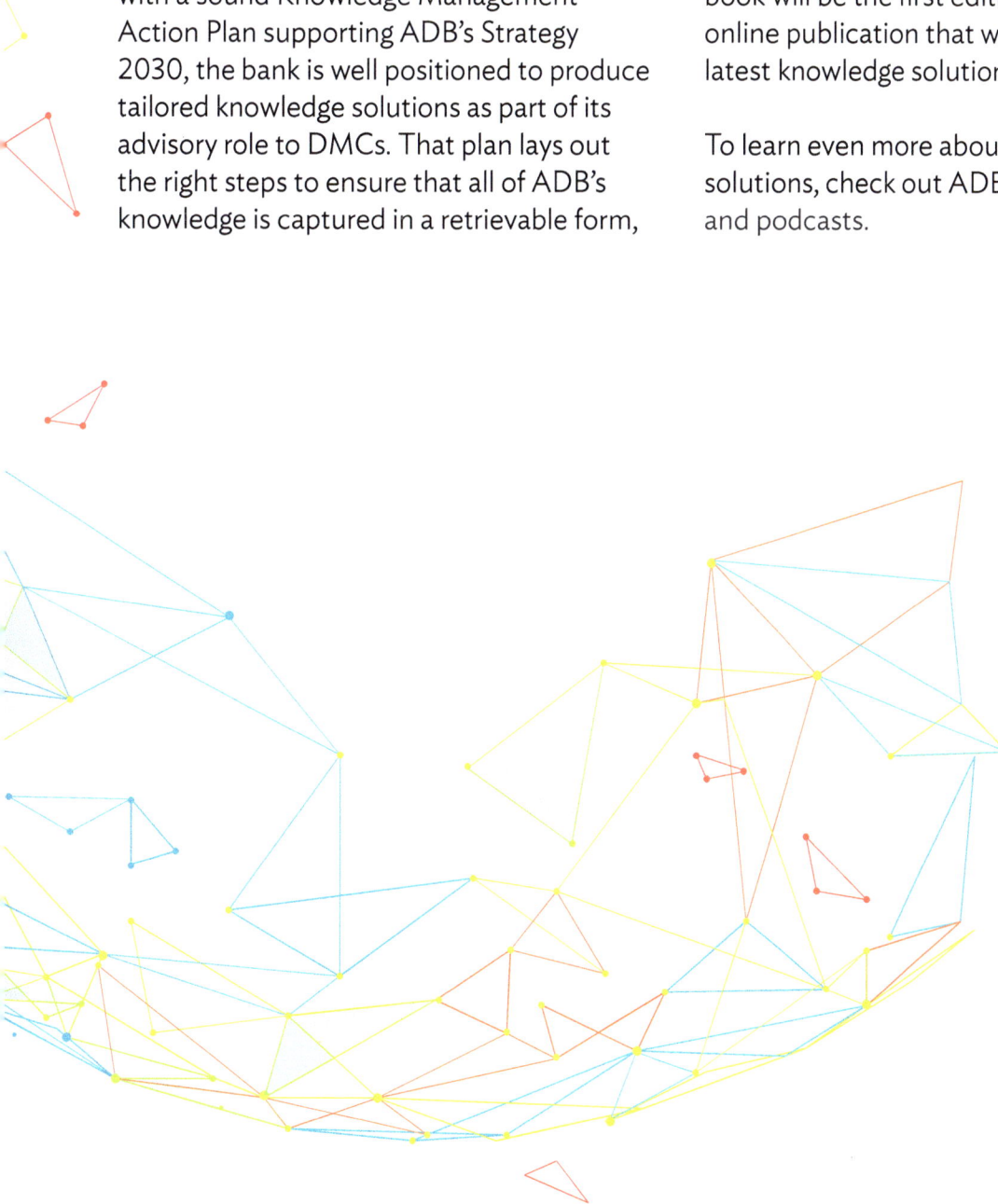

www.ingramcontent.com/pod-product-compliance
Lightning Source LLC
Chambersburg PA
CBHW050042220326
41599CB00045B/7254